This can be completed by the owner, or perhaps in pencil by someone else if the book is a present!

Model:_____

Registration number:_____

Colour:_____

Extras:_____

When purchased:_____

Distinguishing marks/dents/scratches etc:_____

Condition: Excellent ☐ Good ☐ Fair ☐ Bad ☐ Unloved ☐ Other ☐

Most memorable experience in the Vauxhall:_____

Longest journey:_____

Best passenger:_____

Worst passenger:_____

Vauxhall club membership:_____

Other Vauxhall you'd most like to own:_____

Any other comments:_____
_____

Picture:

AFFIX HERE

VAUXHALL

DRIVER'S BOOK

Foulis

Haynes

A **FOULIS** Motoring Book

First published 1990

Published by:
Haynes Publishing Group
Sparkford, Nr Yeovil, Somerset BA22 7JJ

Haynes Publications Inc.
861 Lawrence Drive, Newbury Park, California 91320 USA

British Library Cataloguing in Publication Data
Ruppert, James
    Vauxhall driver's book.
    1.   Cars
    I.   Title
    629.2'222
    ISBN 0-85429-628-X

Library of Congress catalog card number 89-85907

Editor: Mansur Darlington
Page design: Phil Lyons
Page layout: Phil Lyons & Chris Hull
Printed in England by: J.H. Haynes & Co. Ltd

Contents

FORE WORD

Needing wheels, I then bought a Vauxhall Nova 1.2 which was a lively little thing and almost as good as my Cavalier. Unfortunately I swopped it for a small French car that I liked the look of, until things started to drop off. But at least the Nova went to a good home. My parents!

My Vauxhall Cavalier convertible is the best car I've ever owned. It's the same as a BMW, only a lot cheaper and without the yuppie image. People don't tamper with a car like this because they think the owner might kick their heads in!

But my first attempt at running an open-topped car wasn't so successful. After acquiring an old Triumph Vitesse, I gave a plasterer the keys and £100 for his brother to start a restoration. That was the last I saw of the car, the money, or the plasterer.

Of course, Loadsamoney and Stavros wouldn't approve of my Cavalier. Loadsamoney would have an Escort XR3i and Stavros either a boring Ex-cort, or a rusty Peugeot Estate.

Whatever happens though, I'll stick with Vauxhalls for the time being. You'll never find me behind the wheel of a Rolls-Royce because as my granny used to say, they're only driven by pop stars and hairdressers. □

*I*NTRO *D*UCTION

The first car I ever drove was a Vauxhall. Now that's not unusual, but when you consider that I was 18 months old at the time, you'll either be appalled or amazed. However, I must add that my father was operating the pedals and bobbing above dash board level making sure that nothing was in the way.

The jerky progress of this 1956 Wyvern was captured on 8 mm film by the family, but that incriminating evidence has fortunately been mislaid. Not surprisingly, my affection for Vauxhalls has continued, but I didn't really appreciate how popular they were until I was surrounded by dozens of rep-filled Cavaliers on the M4!

Of course the appeal of Vauxhalls today is very different from the early part of this century. Contemporaries with Rolls-Royce, Luton's hand crafted cars were held in the same high esteem. Not only that, Vauxhall dominated motor sport well into the '20s.

Now, Vauxhalls are people's cars. Afford-able, practical and reliable. they have also recaptured many of their former glories, with racing and rallying success.

I hope you enjoy reading The Vauxhall Driver's Book because that's the intention. I'm only trying to reflect the enthusiasm of all the Vauxhall owners and fanatics I've met during the course of compiling this book. You'll even find a Vauxhall Trivia Test at the back of the book to make sure that you've been paying attention.

Whether you've got a new Cavalier, rusty Viva, or restored Cresta, and you enjoy looking at, reading and laughing about all sorts of Vauxhalls there's something in the Vauxhall Drivers Book for you. ☐

James Ruppert

THANX...

Without other people willing to put up with your tiresome phone calls, endless letters and constant requests for photographs, a book like this would be rather thin. So here they are, the people who really need all the thanks.

Dee for encouragement and patience during the compilation of the book. Miriam Carroll at Vauxhall Cars who has been extremely helpful and supportive throughout. The General Motors Photographic Department, Jeremy Phillips at Sylva Autokits, Niall Johnson at Swindon Sportscars, Mr Matchen at Hawk and Brian Mumford at Mumford Engineering for telling me all about their Vauxhall-based kit cars. Edmund & Mario Lindsay, two of the nicest enthusiasts, who spent many patient hours with me. Guy Turner and Adrian Miller who told me all about Vivas. Chris Mateson and Neil Bonner from the F Victor Club. Steve Knight, Richard Angus and Charles Dobres at Lowe Howard Spink for the Ads and all their help. Ashley Kopitko. Bill Blydenstein for being so patient and helpful about the DTV years. Mike Nash from the VX/490 Club. Paul Bramford at Magard. The Opel-Vauxhall Drivers' Club. John Mullen at the Vauxhall Owners' Club. The Droop Snoot Group. Jim Ballie at Fleming Thermodynamics. Mrs Leonora Pearce at the Victor 101 Club. Clive Househam at Street Machine Magazine. Robert Goodchild. Panther Cars. Professor Gustav Foresight for taking time off from his research activites to compile the trivia test. Steve Fellows at Paul Davies Public Relations. Rob Iles and Rod Grainger at Haynes. Mum and Dad for their continuing support. And everyone who has written about Vauxhalls in the past.

And of course anyone else I've shamelessly omitted. I hope they know who they are.

THE *Vauxhall* HERITAGE

Profile: Fulk le Bréant

Roots: Many motor manufacturers can trace their origins back to the 1800s, but very few can go as far back as the 13th century. To understand the origins of Vauxhall we have to meet a very colourful character called Fulk le Bréant.

Lifestyle & Luton: Fulk was a Norman and a mercenary by trade. His main employer was King John for whom he acted as a one man dirty tricks department. In return the grateful King bestowed several honours on Fulk, amongst them Sherriff of Oxford and Hertford, including the Manor of Luton.

Badge: As his heraldic emblem Fulk chose the Griffin, a mythical creature that was half eagle, half lion.

Property: The ambitious Fulk went on to marry a young widow called Margaret de Redvers, who was not only rich, but also had a fine house on the south bank on the Thames.

The connection: For a time it was known as Fulk's hall, but over the years this name was mispronounced and misspelt. From Fulk's to Fawkes, to Fox Hall and finally Vauxhall.

Postcript: Poor old Fulk's luck ran out once King John died. After being exiled to France he died without two francs to rub together.

Vauxhall: 1661: The estate is opened to the public as a pleasure garden. It attracts King Charles, his floozy Nell Gwyn and an entry in

but it was the junction and river that attracted Vauxhall's most famous import.

In 1857 a Scottish engineer, Alexander Wilson, started a business at the Vauxhall Iron Works in south London. The griffin was adopted as the company badge and by 1905 the Vauxhall Car Company had moved to Fulk's old Manor in Luton! Was it fate, or just an incredible series of coincidences? Originally known as Wilson's, the works later became known as 'The Vauxhall'. The rest is history, so read on.

Samuel Pepys' diary. 1733: Impresario John Tyler takes a lease to run the gardens with Frederick Prince of Wales on his management committee. 1859: Gardens sold and the rot sets in, 'tea gardens, then taverns and then disreputable places', whatever that means. The arrival of Vauxhall Junction railway station ddn't help matters appearance-wise,

But before Vauxhall cars there were Wilson's marine engines which powered everything from Admiralty vessels to Thames tugs and the 'Jabberwock' was fitted with the first petrol engine developed by Vauxhall, which was very similar to the original single cylinder unit used on their first car.

When Wilson left in 1894, it was F. W. Hodges, an apprenticed employee, and J. H. Chambers, the company's official receiver, who went on to develop and build the first Vauxhall car in 1903. In the same way that Henry Royce (of Rolls-Royce fame) bought a Decauville to see how cars were built, Hodges did the same. With its rear engine and belt drive that Vauxhall blueprint was probably a Benz. Anyway that first Vauxhall turned out to be quite different from the German car.

The original model and the four-seat version with the two extra passengers placed over the engine ahead of the driver. The output was just 5 hp, with two forward and one reverse gear, transmitted by chain to the rear wheels. What brought the car back to standstill from its 25 mph maximum were leather-lined brakes! Of the 43 examples built just one remains and that can be found in the Science Museum.

For 1904 a new model was launched, the 12/14 hp which had three water-cooled cylinders, as well as three forward speeds and one reverse. Development was rapid as they became more car than horseless carriage, with four seats, steering wheel and bonnet.

As further models were added, Vauxhall urgently needed more production room. So in 1905 they moved the company to Luton, which at the time was a small country town. Pictured above is the works gathering to celebrate production of the Bedfordshire-built cars. This was a significant year for Vauxhall as it saw the introduction of a four-cylinder 18 hp model, which also incorporated their most enduring design feature, the fluted bonnet.

Flutes: Why did Vauxhall decide to use flutes on their models? Vauxhall themselves aren't really sure, but it became such a distinctive part of their cars that it was used on every model from 1905 to 1959. In fact, stylists over the years often found it a burden to incorporate the flutes on every model.

Perhaps the most convincing explanation of how the flutes came about is that put forward by a Luton historian. Apparently a Vauxhall director lying in bed one night began to examine the wardrobe design very closely. A shield carved into the door so impressed him that he made sure similar flutings were adopted on the grille and bonnet of all Vauxhalls.

In 1906 the Vauxhall Iron Works (as it was still called) amalgamated with its close neighbour West Hydraulic Engineering. This new alliance introduced one of Britain's most famous motor engineers to the company and also several new problems. The problem was that they were making too wide a variety of products, from marine engines to hydraulic equipment. So in order to take care of their motoring interests, the Vauxhall Motors Limited was incorporated in 1907. One advantage of specialisation was that they could concentrate on the quality of their products. In the painting and body shop this attention to detail is obvious.

Vauxhall's eagerness to have competition success led directly to the development of the 20 hp type A, which was designed to comply with the 1908 RAC Trials which it won. A more powerful B-Type was introduced in 1909 which seems to have met with the full approval of the constabulary.

Milestone models: The Prince Henry

Development

The 1911 C-Type was based on the cars that Vauxhall entered for the Prussian reliability trials and featured the same pointed nose. Originally offered with 20 hp it acquired a 25 hp unit in 1913. In 1914 its wheelbase grew to 10 ft 10 in.

Importance

It proved to be Vauxhall's most popular production and most successful competition car.

Name

It became known as the 'Prince Henry' after the 1910 Prince Henry of Prussia motor.

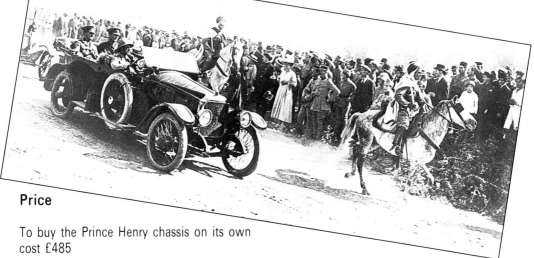

Price

To buy the Prince Henry chassis on its own cost £485

Numbers

190 examples were built

Sum up

Discontinued in 1914 the Prince Henry is generally accepted as being the first British built sports car. Eastern Europe was a very important market for Vauxhall and very popular with the Tsar and the rest of the Royal Family. The big chassis was ideal to take the limousine bodies that the nobility expected. In recognition of the importance of the Russian market, Vauxhall even operated their own, British-staffed outlet in St Petersburg. This is the limousine supplied to the Russian Imperial family in 1914 based on the 35 hp B-Type chassis.

Vauxhall's most enduring car was introduced in 1912, the 25 hp D-Type, which over the following nine years appeared in a variety of body styles. As a money earner it was just what the company needed and proved its worth during the First World War.

The D-Type effectively became the British Army's standard staff car and saw action in all theatres. King George visited the lines at Vimy Ridge in one. The victorious General Allenby entered Jerusalem in a D-Type. And the first car to cross the Rhine into Germany after the Armistice? Of course, a D-Type.

In all, some 2,000 D-Types were built for military purposes, so when the war had finished, Vauxhall had a thoroughly tried and tested model on which to rebuild their reputation.

The company also had another pre-war car on which it could rely. The E-Type, or 30/98, which developed into one of the 'classic' sports cars of the '20s and proved to be unbeatable in competition. The 30/98 came with an unusual and very special guarantee, "This car will reach 100 mph." When it was re-introduced in 1919 prices ranged from £1300 to £1950 depending on the type of bodywork that was ordered.

However, Vauxhall were still producing comparatively expensive and exclusive cars. In an attempt to widen their appeal, the M-Type, or 14/40 tourer, was introduced in 1922 and aimed at the "less sporting" driver. This move pre-empted one of the most important events in Vauxhall's history.

Some of the last 'real' Vauxhalls: an OD Carlton Limousine. The popular "Melton" 2-seater based on the LM.

In December 1925, General Motors paid $2¹/₂ million and acquired their first overseas manufacturing plant. Vauxhall were now part of a multi-national company. For a while they continued to build the big cars that they had become famous for, like the R, S and T types.

By 1930 the first fruits of GM co-operation had become evident. The Vauxhall Cadet was aimed directly at the medium family saloon market. Prices for the new car started at just £250, which was £100 less than a 1904 12/14 had been! The Cadet was available with a six-cylinder engine producing either 17, or 26 hp. But as with all Vauxhalls that had preceded it, a whole host of body styles were on offer from coachbuilders. A year later the Cadet was the first British car to have a synchromesh gearbox, one of many engineering firsts.

Half way through 1933 the Cadet was succeeded by the Light Six, which cost just £180 and almost immediately accounted for 40% of all 14 hp sales in Britain. With this new model Vauxhall rapidly became one of the most successful volume motor manufacturers in the UK. By 1934 output had doubled to 20,000 units a year and the Luton plant now occupied more than 30 acres. More macho stuff from Vauxhall as Light Sixes venture where they really shouldn't.

Vauxhall growth through the 1930s continued and was due to the foresight of the managing board who decided to invest £1,000,000 in the important, but highly competitive 10 hp market.

Milestone Models: The '10'

People

In the 1930s there were many vehicles that claimed to be people's cars. But when Vauxhall entered the 10 hp market in 1937 they produced a car that unlike the competition wasn't small and crude.

Advanced

With the 10, also known as the H-type, Vauxhall became the first British manufacturer to build a car on the integral construction principle, or monocoque as it is now known. Without a separate chassis the body becomes the frame. Another innovation, independent front suspension, set new standards for small car handling.

Benefits

During the frugal Thirties much was also made of the car's exceptional fuel consumption figures that averaged over 40 mpg. And the performance (50 mph +) was impressive too.

Popular

With a price tag of just £168, it came as no surprise that more than 10,000 were sold in the first five months of production. In just three years 55,000 examples were sold.

Legacy

The 10 allowed Vauxhall to grow and also prove that they were one of the most advanced motor manufacturers in the world. In fact, it took some car makers more than 20 years to catch up with some of the 10's features. Today every mass-produced car conforms to the basic construction principles of the 10.

By 1938 the ten thousandth Vauxhall 10 had been sold and the company added a larger companion model, the 12 hp I-Type, which strengthened their position in the medium car market. However, motor car production all but stopped as Vauxhall joined the war effort.

Although they didn't build many cars during the hostilities (just 100) Vauxhall

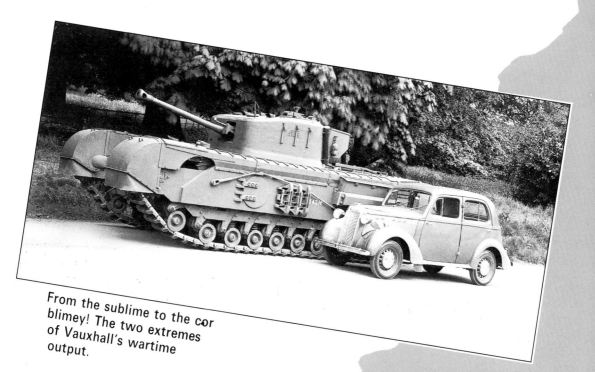

From the sublime to the cor blimey! The two extremes of Vauxhall's wartime output.

certainly made up for it with their Bedford Trucks (250,000), such as the four wheel drive QL.

Perhaps Luton's most impressive achievement during this period was designing and building a tank from scratch! Just one year after receiving the commission in 1940, the famous 38 ton Churchill tank was entering

active service.

Of course, Luton did not escape the ravages of war and in the worst raid, sadly, 39 workers were killed.

However, Vauxhall's contribution went beyond making vehicles. Shells, small arms, jerry cans and aircraft were either built, or developed by the experts at Luton. These projects even included the research and implementation of the jet engine.

When peace came and normal production was resumed, the new models were not jet powered. Vauxhall had to re-introduce their pre-war range until they had built up the resources to fund new cars. It was the L models in 1948 that resurrected an old name

Velox (as used on the 1913 30/98) and introduced a new one, the Wyvern. These all-new models triggered off a huge demand for Vauxhall products and in order to cope, a major expansion programme costing £14 million was initiated. The result was a brand new 19½ acre plant at Luton and a growing Vauxhall range.

At their 1953 Golden Jubilee there was much to celebrate: a popular line-up, which now included the Cresta, a luxury version of the Velox and production that now topped 100,000 units a year.

By 1957 the brand new F-Type Victors rapidly became one of Britain's most successful exports and was later modified to become Vauxhall's first estate car. That year also marked the return of the "big" Vauxhall with the American-influenced PA Velox and Cresta.

Profile: David Jones

Early years

Joined Vauxhall in 1934 from the Royal College of Art simply to earn enough to finance a holiday in France.

Style

Stayed once he found that making models for future designs was enjoyable. So immediately became the Styling Department.

1959 was the real watershed year for the company as it produced the millionth Vauxhall and deleted the distinctive bonnet flutes that had survived for fifty years.

Vauxhall entered the sixties with confidence as the company grew with a major new plant at Ellesmere Port in Liverpool, which was followed by a new parts centre, styling department and proving ground at Millbrook. Much of their success was due to Vauxhall's decision to re-enter the small car market with the 1 litre Viva.

America

Part of his apprenticeship involved spending sometime at General Motors. This undoubtedly influenced his designs from then on.

Chrome

From the 1953 Wyvern, Velox and Cresta models on Jones's scaled-down American cars were in total contrast to the cars of the day. His 'big' car influence survived with the Crestas and Victors into the '70s.

Sum up

Responsible for some of the most distinctive designs to emerge from a British manufacturer.

Milestone Models: 'Viva'

Small

When Vauxhall decided to re-enter the small car market, they did so with one of the most popular model ranges of the '60s and '70s.

Features

The HA Viva had a lively one litre engine, a square but modern body and a very spacious interior. It proved to be an instant success.

Successful

After just ten months of production more than 100,000 Vivas had been built which played a large part in Vauxhall's record figures for 1964. By 1966 there were more than 300,000 happy owners of HAs. The familiar boxy shape of the original Viva HA lived on in the Bedford Van until 1984!

More models

If the HA had been successful, then the HB models did even better. With even more room inside and a new stylish body it was no surprise that 500,000 examples had found good homes by 1970. Four doors, the Brabham and GT, went on to widen the model's appeal. In the '70s more derivatives like the Magnum and Firenza confirmed that the Viva had become the UK's most popular and adaptable saloon.

Sum up

Vauxhall's most important post-war model.

At the up-market end of things Vauxhall maintained its big car presence with the Crestas and Viscounts. The whole range was updated with almost American regularity. Here's the changing face of the Vauxhall Victor. 1961–64 FB. 1964–67 FC. 1967–72 FD. 1972–76 renamed VX and discontinued in 1978.

Profile: Wayne Cherry

Early years

Studied at The Los Angeles Art School. Joined Vauxhall in the mid-Sixties.

The Droop

What brought Cherry worldwide recognition was the Droop Snoot look. He led the styling team which produced this concept which was readily accepted by senior management and put into production. Not only did it do away with the traditional grille, it also dramatically reduced wind resistance.

Hatchback

Recognising the benefits and practicality of a rear door, Cherry made sure that the Chevette range included hatchback alternatives. As a result General Motors implemented the concept across their entire range both in Europe and the US.

DRG

Cherry is credited with creating the phrase "down-the-road-graphics" which means how the car looks on the street. He was one of the first to realize the importance of subtle body modifications such as skirts and spoilers. These haven't always been copied successfully by others.

Enthusiast

Unlike a lot of corporate men he does have a genuine love of cars, having owned many Ferraris and of course styling his own prototypes for road use.

Sum up

A designer who really has influenced the way all cars look today. Look around you, there are droop snoots and hatchbacks everywhere. By the mid-Seventies Vauxhall recognised the need to up-date their range and embarked on an ambitious programe of model introduction. The practical Chevette was introduced in 1975 and quickly established itself in the small car market. That same year Vauxhall introduced the Cavalier, a car that would overtake and effectively replace the Viva in importance.

Milestone Models: The Cavalier

Introduction

The Cavalier was basically the British version

of the Opel Ascona. But it was more than simply a badge change. The droop snoot design, highly original at the time has since become a standard design feature of many modern cars.

Rep mobile

Reliability, practicality with a touch of style have made the Cavalier the travelling rep's choice.

Update

With the '81 model came a totally new body and front wheel drive which pushed it to the top of the sales chart.

Sum up

The first effective rival to Ford Cortina and Vauxhall's most successful car of the '80s and probably the '90s too.

It was the company's 75th anniversary, the future looked bright, but what exactly would the next decades hold for Vauxhall? To find out you'll have to skip a few pages and read about Vauxhall Today.   □

Motor Sport

Vauxhall have always been closely involved with motorsport. Most of the time they have been content to modify their road-going cars, aware that competition success results in more sales of their production models.

As soon as Vauxhalls were being hand built, they were being entered for reliability trials that were popular in the early part of this century. Vauxhall had such faith in their 6 hp

1904 model that they entered it for the gruelling Glasgow to London run. Despite being the smallest car entered it finished with only seven points lost out of a possible thousand! And that was to change a faulty plug.

Not only did Vauxhall have reliable cars on its side, it also had the foremost motoring racing drivers and engineers of the day

Scrutineers make sure that the Vauxhall meets with the trial's regulations.

steering them to victory. A.J. Hancock and Percy Kidner were both executives and drivers for Vauxhall. At the 1908 2,000 mile trial Kidner piloted a 20 hp Vauxhall designed by the brilliant engineer Laurence Pomeroy. Yet again the car lost fewer marks than any other competitor. This highly successful car came into being because the chief engineer was on holiday in Egypt and the Board decided to build a new Vauxhall around the 1908 RAC trial rules.

In 1909 Vauxhall made the ambitious decision to specifically build a car for record breaking purposes. Called the KN it resembled a torpedo and rapidly proved the company right. With Hancock at the wheel the car powered round the Brooklands track breaking the flying half mile (at 88.6 mph) and distance (ten laps at 81.33 mph) records. The speed record followed just a year later when the car achieved 100.08 mph.

When in 1910 Prince Henry of Prussia sponsored a rally intended as a demanding test for standard touring cars, the 20 hp Type A, with a distinctive pointed radiator for this event, proved ideal. The three-car team displayed remarkable performance and reliability during the tour and then led directly to

KN rolling into action at Brooklands. Note man in background getting ready for the post-race victory party with a crate of best.

the development of the famous Prince Henry Vauxhalls.

For the Swedish Winter Trial in 1912, not surprisingly held in freezing conditions (at

Again in 1913 Vauxhall and Pomeroy designed a car specifically for a race (the Shelsley Hill Climb). The result was that the E-type or 30/98, a 4-cylinder side valve with a special aluminium body, won that event in record time. In fact, that record was to stand for the next 15 years. Not long after, a similar car also increased the Brooklands lap speed to 103.76 mph. The 30/90 went on to spearhead Vauxhall's racing challenge into the next decade and was one of the most successful sports cars of the 1920s, even though it didn't get front brakes until 1926!

Vauxhall's foray into Grand Prix racing was a disappointment. Between 1913 and 1914 and despite an increase in capacity from 3.3 to 4$^{1/2}$ litre the specially built two-seaters failed to shine.

Vauxhall's re-entry into racing was slow and never really sanctioned by the factory, although there were of course private entries like these:

times 40°F below), two Prince Henrys were entered and one of them went on to score an impressive victory. In 1913 alone, both works and privately owned Prince Henrys won 35 hill climbs, 23 Brooklands victories and 14 reliability trials.

Officially, Vauxhall withdrew from motor sport in 1924, having established their cars as one of the premier sporting marques. It was also very expensive!

PA Cresta on the Monte
Carlo Rally receiving a wash
and brush up. It didn't win.

Although Bill Blydenstein started Vauxhall's racing revival with the VX4/90, he soon transferred to the Viva which had much more potential.

Viva – early days:

As an alternative to tuning Minis, Blydenstein turned his attention to the original HA Viva in which he won several class awards at sprint meetings. However, it was the HB that offered more room for development and in 1967 began work on Shaw and Kilburn's (Vauxhall dealers) Vivas.

Early drivers:

Blydenstein, an accomplished driver, was joined by fellow Dutchman Han Akersloot for a time before recruiting someone to take over track duties whilst he concentrated on preparing the cars. That someone was the legendary Gerry Marshall.

Early Cars:

The original Viva had a 1258 cc unit producing 95 bhp and a very heavy body that didn't help, although class wins were achieved. However, once the GT arrived in 1968 with its 2 litre overhead camshaft engine, and when fuel injection was added, the results began to change. At the end of '69 Marshall was runner up in the Saloon Car Championship.

Overseas:

In 1970 Blydenstein had the task of returning Vauxhall to international competition after a very long absence. This meant combining British club racing with International Group 2 with a 2 litre Viva GT. A fourth at Spa was particularly impressive.

Success:

In 1971 Vivas won all the major saloon car championships.

Here they are gathered together at Ellesmere Port: (left to right) Des Donnelly, Irish saloon-car champion, Jim Thompson BARC hill climb champion, Bill Dryden, Scottish saloon-car champion and Gerry Marshall, Osram/GEC special saloon-car champion.

Familiar sight for the Shaw and Kilburn Vivas and a depressing one for all Escorts.

A Blydenstein-prepared Viva gives some BMWs a hard time on ice. In fact the Viva team became Swedish ice racing champions in 1971 proving just how versatile these cars were.

Power:

Although a number of engine options 2.2, 2.3, 2.5 and 2.6, the team eventually settled on the 2.3 litres producing 240 bhp.

Nickname:

'Old Nail' – because it was a consistent, reliable winner.

First season:

The Thames TV Firenza scored two firsts and took the lap record on its debut at Llandow. In all it amassed 9 outright wins out of 23 races.

Second season:

Things went even better with a 2.5 litre unit. Gerry Marshall won the Forward Trust Championship with 1F wins. However things didn't always go so smoothly.

Rallying:

Although nicely balanced the Firenza was always too heavy and not quite agile enough to be a really successful rally weapon. However, they were a regular sight in '70s events and always did well in their class.

Success:

The revised car brought 21 wins, 3 lap records and a class title in the Forward Trust series.

Development: In 1973 the Firenza acquired a Lotus 2.2 engine with 16-valve cylinder head, 5-speed ZF gearbox, a dry sump, wider rear wheels and a lump on the bonnet to house the injection trumpets.

Droop snoot racer:

The most obvious body modifications were made at the end of the year – the new nose cone and spoiler added up to the 'droop snoot look'.

In a special 'Snoots only' race Gerry Marshall takes an unsuccessful short cut across the turf to overtake Barry 'Whizzo' Williams. Several similar manoeuvres later he took the lead and won.

V8s

V8 Ventora

Nickname:

'Big Bertha' – because it was big.

Birth:

Intended as both a show and racing car to promote a proposed road-going V8 version of the Ventora.

Details:

Space frame tubular construction, part steel, part glassfibre body powered by a 5 litre Holden V8 engine.

Verdict:

Very fast, but almost unmanageably heavy to drive. However, Gerry Marshall managed 3 wins out of 6 races.

Death:

In its last outing at Silverstone Big Bertha was reduced to scrap.

V8 Firenza:

Nickname:

'Baby Bertha' – basically because it was the offspring of 'Bertha.'

The car:

From the wreckage of 'Big Bertha', the 'Baby' emerged with the V8 unit shoehorned into the Firenza bodyshell.

Baby Bertha undergoing its one and only engine failure.

Success:

Mondello in Ireland was the scene of Baby's first win. But perhaps the most significant victory was at the British Grand Prix support race where Gerry Marshall averaged 110 mph and finished 38 seconds ahead of the nearest car. The Tricentrol Super Saloon titles followed in '75 and '76. It was retired in '77.

Verdict:

Undoubtedly the best of the track racing Vauxhalls, almost purpose-built for Gerry Marshall it deservedly dominated the mid '70s.

Profile: Gerry Marshall

32

Early years:

Gerald Dallas Royston Marshall was born into a rural environment which meant that he could play with tractors and other mechanical objects at an absurdly young age. Mopeds and motorcycles followed eventually culminating in his first four-wheeled car, a Ford Popular.

Early racing:

Swopping a restored Riley for a less than pristine racing mini, but it was the start of his career. A succession of minis followed, although his last one was sold to pay for an engagement ring! That of course wouldn't stop him racing and more minis popped up along with interesting drives in Lotus Elans and TVRs.

Vauxhalls:

Marshall meets Blydenstein. The rest is history and can be read elsewhere.

The man:

Basically larger than life, certainly physically. Marshall has always displayed charisma by the bucketful ready to laugh and tell a good story. Apparently Marshall has always enjoyed the occasional social drink, but this has never been confirmed.

The driver:

Certainly one of the best in the world when it comes to saloon cars. His outstanding second place (with Peter Brock) in the 1977 Spa 24 hours confirms this. His control is total, although his low centre of gravity probably helps! Always concerned that racing should be fun, rather than dominate a race Marshall would make a sudden pit stop so that he could enjoy fighting his way back into the lead a lap later!

Sum up:

One of the great British drivers of the last few decades. Along with Bill Blydenstein he put Vauxhalls back on the international racing map. Not only that, he did it with a smile on his face. That familiar sideways driving style will probably never be forgotten.

CHEVETTE

Anatomy of a Vauxhall Rally Car.

Vauxhall withdraw shock:

The astonishing decision was made to switch from racing and concentrate on international rallying where it was felt that the company's profile would be higher and the impact greater.

Specifications:

HS 2.3 litre engine with Lotus cylinder head producing 240 bhp, triple plate clutch and ZF 5-speed gearbox. Body modifications included spoilers and wheel arch extensions.

Success:

In its first year of competition, Pentti Airikkala and Chris Sclater won two international rallies and finished second in the British Championship. In the next season they won four more rallies and Airikkala became British Champion.

HSR:

Introduced in 1980 the engine produced 245 bhp with a Getrag 5-speed gearbox. Bonnet, boot lid, front/rear wing extensions and sills are now made of fibreglass.

Nicknames:

Often referred to as the 'Silver Bullet', or 'Silver Rollerskate'.

Retired:

1984 was the last season, although the Chevette was beginning to find it hard work against the Quattro. Increasingly more money and development effort was being channelled into the Opel side of competition with GM Dealer Sport.

Success II:
Circuit of Ireland with Jimmy McRae at the wheel. Terry Kaby took the National title and Drew Gallagher the Scottish. In '81 there were more wins, Vauxhall taking the manufacturer's award.

Sum up:

The Chevette was undoubtedly Vauxhall's finest rally car. Powerful, agile and – in the right driver's hands – unbeatable.

Profile: Bill Blydenstein

Very early years:

He was born Willem Benjamin Blydenstein of
Dutch and Norwegian parents.

Early racing years:

A Saloon Car champion in 1960, he raced a
number of cars from Minis to Borgwards. But
not only did he drive, Blydenstein also
prepared the cars. He later switched to
Vauxhall and campaigned VX4/90s then in
1965 the HA Viva. Then Gerry Marshall took
over the driving duties in 1969. The rest is
history and can be read elsewhere.

Success:

Blydenstein has been involved with every
important Vauxhall victory since 1970
whether racing (130 outright wins both here
and abroad) or rallying (20 international wins
alone).

Tuning:

It's impossible to separate the name of
Blydenstein from fast Vauxhalls. The range
and effectiveness of the modified cylinder
heads, camshafts, etc., means that Blydenstein is the first stop for anyone wanting to
make their Vauxhall more potent, or VW, or
Datsun, or Ford, or Honda, or . . .

Legacy:

Thanks to Bill Blydenstein the Vauxhall
regained its sporting heritage.

1982 GM Dealer Sport:

Formed at the beginning of 1982 along
similar lines to DTV with the dealers still
providing a significant proportion of the
backing.

VAUXHALL Rally Drivers

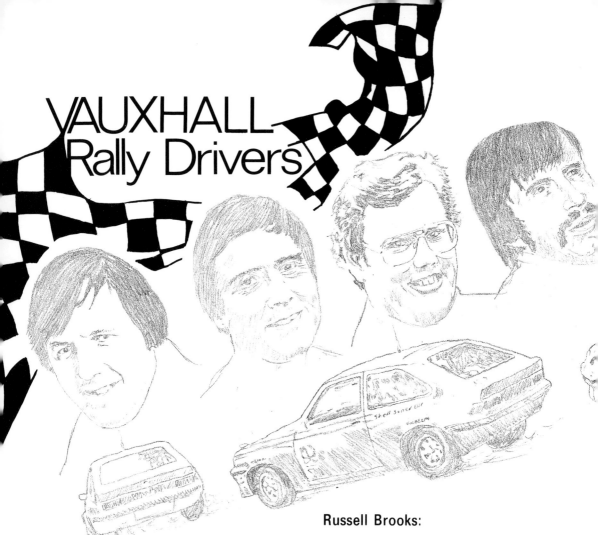

Jimmy McRae:

Originally a highly competitive rider on motorcycles for more than 12 years he drove Group One Vauxhalls between 1975 and '78 then Chevettes until '81. Ironically 1980 was his best year as he won four rallies, Vauxhall's only victories, before DTV financial restrictions meant that there was no place for him the following season. However, he joined Opel and has never looked back as International success has continued.

Russell Brooks:

One of Britain's most experienced and successful drivers, Brooks joined the Chevette team in '82. Unfortunately this was the beginning of the 4WD era. However, determined driving meant that he never failed to finish a race below fourth place. His persistence was rewarded in 1983 with an outstanding Circuit of Ireland victory.

Pentti Airikkala:

Began racing Vauxhall Magnums, but left to rally Escorts and was only attracted back by the arrival of the Chevette HS. He scored DTV's first international victory in the Welsh rally. Establishing himself as Vauxhall's leading driver he secured the British Championship in 1979.

Will Sparrow:

With a Magnum prepared by Coburn Improvements, Sparrow helped with Vauxhall's entry into the rally scene, becoming National Rally Champion in 1973. Soldiering on with the heavy Magnum he did manage 9th place in the 1975 RAC Rally, leading Vauxhall to the team prize. He briefly made it into the Chevette era with the first competitive drive of an HS in '76.

Terry Kaby:

As one of Britain's most respected club racers his move to Chevettes brought immediate success when in 1980 he won the National Rally Championship. The good results continued in '81 with a win in the Manx and high placings in other events.

Tony Pond:

Having gained racing experience in 16-valve Vauxhall-engined Chevairs for GM in South Africa and being soundly beaten by them on home ground when he drove for British Leyland, Pond eagerly joined DTV in '81. Arguably the best of Chevette HSR exponents Pond claimed five outright victories in just one season with the team.

...and the CARS

Astra GTE

Success:

The Astra has taken over from the Chevette HS and has an impressive record of victories.

Pre-GTE:

Even in the early days the Astra proved that it had the makings of a fine rally car by winning its class in the 1981 & 1982 Open Rally Championships.

GTE:

1984 Group N and A winners. 1985 Group A and N win and RAC Rally Group A. 1986 Group A National Rally Champions. 1987 Group A and N winners.

Car: Nova

Success:

Perhaps an unlikely winner, but nonetheless, the plucky little car really has dominated its class. 1984–85–86–87 1300 Group A Class.

Car: Carlton Thundersaloon

Track:

The Carlton Thundersaloon in 1986 represented Vauxhall's return to circuit racing with quite a degree of vengeance and noise! Winning 8 races, they proved that Luton were serious. Could this be 'Baby Bertha' all over again?

Derek Bell

One of Britain's most successful drivers of all time has been closely involved with the racing side of Vauxhall for the last few years. Derek Bell has raced just about every type of car from Formula One to Sports Prototypes. In fact, Le Mans has become his second home, winning more times there than anyone else.

Vauxhall have given him the opportunity to race in even more diverse events. To date he's been a regular behind the wheel of the Thundersaloon and also a rally-prepared Astra where he's been finding his feet on the loose surface, but still managing impressive displays.

James Hunt

Winner of the 1973 Tour of Britain was James Hunt – in a Vauxhall. Not a great many people realise that!

VAUXHALL VLOTUS
CHALLENGE

If you thought that all the skill involved in racing cars had disappeared with Fangio and Moss in the '50s you're probably right. These days it often seems that the team with the most money always holds the technical advantage and all the faceless pilots have to do is switch on the engine and win.

However, Vauxhall have decided to change all that with a unique single seat racing formula that has effectively put every driver and team back on equal terms.

The car:

Designed – Adrian Reynard with chassis by Lotus.

Chassis – consists of two sandwich section side members (6′ x 1′ x 2″) bolted to an aluminium casting at the front, which then locates the wishbones, and to a 5-speed Hewland Transaxle at the rear. A tubular frame forming the roll-bar and steering mount is bolted on top and an aluminium plate beneath.

Safety – behind the seat is a 30 litre bag fuel tank and a 7.5 kg fire extinguishing system. Frontal crush zone, side impact pontoons.

Body – One piece cockpit/engine cover, nose cone and front aerofoil, a rear aerofoil and side pods that withstand side impact and also housing radiator and dry sump catch tank.

Suspension – double wishbones with inboard spring/damper units.

Brakes – ventilated discs.

Wheels – Techno magnesium alloy wheels Front: 6 x 13 Rear 8 x 13.

Engine – 1998 cc, four-cylinders, 16-valves, Twin choke side-draught Weber DCOEs, bore/stroke 86 x 86 mm, compression ratio 10.5:1. BHP 155.

If you still can't afford to take part in the racing, you could always buy a 16V Astra GTE!

The rules:

* The cars are built to a single design which provides economical racing and uniform performance.

* Engines are produced on the standard production line. The fuel injection equipment is removed to prevent tampering.

* The bottom half of the engine is rebuilt for dry sump lubrication, test run for an hour and then lock wired and sealed.

* Each team is only allowed one spare engine.

* Each engine is checked by GM for output.

* Repair is by replacement so that no unlawful modifications take place.

* Only six slick tyres are allowed per event, to ensure that this happens tyres have been registered and coded.

* Specifications have been "frozen" for 3 years (from '88) which means that no expensive seasonal updates need to be made.

PERFORMANCE VAUXHALLS

Building fast cars came naturally to Vauxhall in the early part of the century whether it was winning races or setting records. Here are some of the specials and limited editions produced by the factory that have a right to the title of fast Vauxhalls.

The first Vauxhall sports car and indeed the first British sports car of any kind was the D-Type. The next fast Vauxhall was the 30/98.

THE 100 MPH CAR

Date: October 1910
Driver: A.J. Hancock
Car: 20 hp special
Record: The first 20 hp car to exceed 100 mph.

The '30/98' story

Birth

But for Mr. J. Higginson, inventor of the Autovac fuel pump system, the most successful and famous Vauxhall of all would never have been built. Higginson was a leading motor racing competitor when in March 1913 he approached Laurence Pomeroy and asked him to come up with a British sportscar which he could use at the Shelsley Walsh hill climb. That event was just 13 weeks away!

Parts

Pomeroy rummaged around the spare parts bin and came up with a Prince Henry Engine which he enlarged to 4526 cc. This Higginson Special also featured a slim aluminium body with no doors and a rounded radiator.

Race

When it came to the race, Higginson was the clear winner and set a course record that would last for the next 15 years! The 30/98 went on to win more than 75 races and set numerous records.

Name

The biggest mystery has always been how the car gained its name, especially as the engine was neither a 30 hp nor 98 bhp unit. Some attribute it to a long-forgotten mechanic who, for reasons of his own, so christened it '30/98'.

Sum up

Confirmed Vauxhall's reputation as a builder of high performance quality cars.

Over the page ...

Top:

The famous Silver Arrow 30/98 belonging to Major Ropner pictured in 1922, just after a practical demonstration of the 100 mph performance that was "guaranteed" with every example. What's missing is the famous flutes (similar to the Grand Prix cars), though an earlier sports body managed to retain them.

bottom:

Still chasing up the Shelsley Walsh 16 years later in the hands of Raymond Mays.
  During the late '20s and '30s sporting coachwork was of course grafted on to various chassis, but there was no official performance Vauxhall for over 30 years.

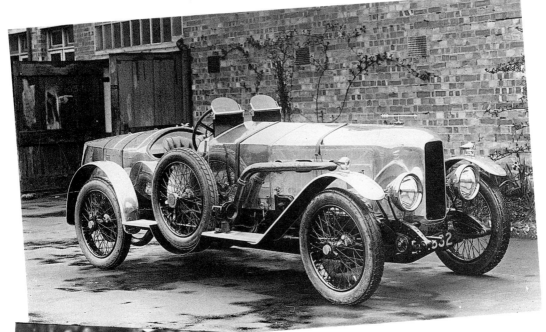

44

VX4/90s

Development

The wait was over with the arrival of VX4/90 which was based on the FB model Victors and introduced in 1962. The decision to build a high performance saloon was based on the simple principle that there was a demand for it. The Victor was chosen because it could be modified and generally uprated without losing the advantages of cost-effective mass production. Although Vauxhall planned to build just 1,000 a month, this figure had to be increased rapidly.

Details

It had twin carburettors, 71 bhp, high compression engine, servo front disc brakes and floor-mounted gearchange.

Performance

With 44% more power than the standard Victor, and increased to 1595 cc, 85 bhp for the '64 models, it could reach 90 mph.

Identifying features

Individual rather than bench seating, slatted grille and prominent side stripe.

This is the cheeky wave that other drivers got as the FB VX4/90s left them standing.

This is the 1967 FC with driver transferring to the only other conveyance with the same thrill factor.

Top right:
FE: 1972 2300 cc engine with twin carbs. Flutes return. Mph now hits three digits!

FD: 1969 Back by popular demand after a two year gap. This time with twin Stromberg carburettors and overdrive. Rostyle wheels, stone guards on the lower rear wheel arches and single bar grille. Automatic offered for the first time. Big car had trouble touching 100 mph though.

Vivas

Brabham
In early '67 a Jack Brabham conversion became available for the '90. What this involved was twin carburettors, and a straight-through exhaust. The result was 79 bhp and a top speed in the higher 80s. Cosmetically wide rim wheels and a Brabham stripe made it look slightly different. These conversions were offered by Vauxhall dealers, after delivery, rather than straight from the factory.

With its light body and agile handling the Viva left plenty of room for performance development.

The Viva 90 HA was introduced in 1965 and based on the de luxe version. Under the bonnet was a high compression engine with revised manifold, strengthened propshaft and Stromberg carburettor that boosted output to 60 bhp. The speedometer would on occasion show 80 plus figures.

Viva GT

This beast came straight from the factory and its matt black grille, twin scoops and wide Rostyle wheels looked as though the car meant business. The new FE Victor's 2 litre overhead camshaft engine with twin Stromberg carbs was dropped in place. Other Victor transplants included the rear axle and of course brakes, to put a stop to its 104 bhp and 100+ top speed.

THE DR**OO**P SN**OO**T STORY

Debut

Earls Court Motor Show October 1973. Centrepiece of the Vauxhall stand. The car on display was only a bog standard Firenza with the usual 1159 cc engine. Official name was the Firenza high performance coupé.

Development

Wayne Cherry produced a number of concept cars. Orange Car was simply a no-frills high performance Firenza with a rear spoiler.

VXD 594M

49

Nose Cone One

This evolved the Droop Snoot look. The Daytona had quarter bumpers and revised bonnet and the very black Black Knight.

Design

Glass fibre panel angled from bonnet to the bumper. Behind flat glass panes were the headlights and below bumper was a glassfibre spoiler. Colour was always silver with matt black window surrounds.

Brains

Many people were involved in the development of the Droop Snoot including stylist Wayne Cherry and engineer Roy Cook.

Power

2.3 litre unit with 9.2:1 compression ratio, larger valves, modified cylinder head, high lift camshaft, twin Stromberg carburettors and special exhaust manifold, lightened flywheel, Ventora clutch and ZF 5-speed gearbox. The result was 131 bhp, a 0–60 time of just over 8 seconds and a top speed that nudged 120 mph.

Handling

Ventora disc brakes and lowered suspension with stiffer springs and gas-filled rear dampers. This was combined with wide 185/70 tyres on 13 inch alloy wheels.

Hot hatch

The Sportshatch appeared at the '74 Motor Show. It offered the same package as the

coupé but with estate car practicality. However, the engine was standard Firenza although 100 plus performance was still possible. Never officially price-listed but 200 examples were built all the same.

Sum up

The most stylish and most copied design that emerged from Luton. A modern classic.

CHEVETTE HS

Birth

The man responsible for most of the fastest Vauxhalls is Bill Blydenstein. And when Vauxhall switched from track racing to rallying Blydenstein proposed that the lightest car be combined with the most powerful engine. This meant a Chevette mated to the Magnum's 2.3 unit.

Homologation

400 cars in 12 months needed to be built in order to qualify for Group 4 competition. Roy Cook was made the project chief to make all this happen, which meant rummaging around the parts bin.

400

November 1976. Building such a small number of cars on a production line was not easy and the launch of the car was delayed by some months. HS not on sale until April '78.

Specification

HS – 2.3 litre engine. 16-valve cylinder head and five-speed Getrag gearbox. 135 bhp. Body additions were glassfibre spoilers. HSR – As HS plus revised engine producing 150 bhp. Body additions side skirts.

Vauxhall

Although there were certain pieces of Opel technology in the Chevette, the HS is regarded as perhaps the last home, or Luton-grown Vauxhall.

Name

It is a mystery as to what the HS stands for. Some say High Speed, others Homologation Special. And the HSR, R for Rally presumably. Any other suggestions?

Sum up

Vauxhall's rally car in road going trim. The hottest hatchback of them all? Exciting stuff!

GTE

Vauxhall's re-entry into the mass-produced fast car market was with the Astra-based GTE.

And if you want to go further than the 'standard' performance offerings from Vauxhall, there are plenty of other options. From bolt-on extras to fully re-engineered cars – the choice is yours.

1983 1.8 litre unit produced 115 bhp. During the Mark 1's production life to '84 it also acquired stiffer suspension and close ratio gearbox. Sports seats, front and rear spoiler distinguished it from the normal model

1985 GTE Mark 2 with an all-new body shape with colour keyed spoilers and door mirrors and alloy wheels. A five-door version was also offered. 1986 GTE now available as SRi. 1987 new GTE 2.0 litre producing 124 bhp.

1988 Nova GTE. Basically a 1.6i producing 100 bhp. There's also stiffer suspension larger steel wheels 14 x 5 and a close ratio gearbox to turn this Nova into a real pocket rocket that'll reach 117 mph!

At the time of going to press, fast Cavaliers were on the way. 2.0 GSi with 16 valve and four wheel drive versions in the pipeline.

Blydenstein

The Blydenstein range of performance packs are probably the best way of making your Vauxhall more responsive. After all, it was Bill Blydenstein who started tinkering with Vauxhalls way back in the '60s.

Not only do the Blydenstein packs boost performance, they do so smoothly and efficiently which means that there are no fuel consumption penalties.

Stage 1: A basic tuning kit for fuel injected cars which improves the induction system and increases power by 4–5%.

A Pack: A carefully gas-flowed and matched cylinder head/valve assembly giving 10–12% power increase.

B Pack: In addition to the A Pack mods, inlet valve size is increased adding 2–3 bhp.

Exhaust & manifold systems: Jetex free-flowing systems boost the bhp output of the A and B Packs.

Here's the *Street Machine* Magazine project Astra. On the outside is a specially designed bodykit from Skeete Auto Design. Underneath the skin is a Blydenstein 'A' Pack along with a Jetex exhaust system. [Photo courtesy *Street Machine* Magazine]

Irmscher

Virtually tuners by appointment to Opel in Germany, not surprisingly they do exactly the same for the Vauxhall range. After Irmscher started breathing life into race and rally saloons back in '68, customers were soon queuing up for similar miracles to be performed on road cars. Irmscher offer both body kits and re-manufactured Vauxhalls with impressive performance modifications. The possible component combinations are almost endless but here's a summary of what they do for each model.

Irmscher Nova

Fuel injection kit/performance camshaft/oil cooler kit/modified exhaust and manifold. Chassis kits which can lower car by 25 mm. Limited slip differential. Revised final drive ratio to 4.18:1.

Irmscher Carlton

Twin carburettor for 2.0 litre engines. Performance Kit consists of modified camshaft, valve springs, tappets, oil return pipe, distributor and sport exhaust. Suspension kits modify springs and shock absorbers.

Irmscher Senator

Engine capacity increased to 3.6 litres, re-programmed Bosch injection system, modified exhaust, revised suspension. With these changes 140 mph isn't out of the question.

Irmscher Astra

Twin side draught carburettor/fuel injection unit for 1300 models, Turbo unit available for 1.8, performance camshaft, reinforced valve springs, oil cooler/modified exhaust and manifold. Chassis kits replace shock absorbers and springs and can lower suspension by 25 mm.

Irmscher Cavalier

Sport camshaft, reinforced valve springs, limited slip differential. Chassis kits replace shock absorbers and springs, lowering suspension by 25 mm.

55

Courtenay's

Norfolk-based General Motors dealer Courtenay's have teamed up with Pace Products to produce a turbo option for the complete Vauxhall range, using intercooled IHI turbochargers.

Courtenay Nova

Here's the engine compartment of the 1.3 Nova and here's the Turbo. This package produces 120 bhp and 125 mph top speed. The 1600 GTE has a further 25 bhp power boost.

Courtenay Astra & Cavalier

1600 versions will produce 135 bhp and 130 mph. 1800i 147 bhp and 127 mph. 2.0i 155 bhp and 130 mph+.

Courtenay Carlton & Senator

3.0 225 bhp and speeds around the 150 mph mark!

Courtenay's are always willing to produce a car finished to your own exact requirements. This not only includes the engine, but also body kits.

Turbo Technics Astra GTE

One of the most respected names in turbo charging, Turbo Technics employ a Garett T3 unit. A combination of machined pistons, replacement camshaft and specially manufactured head gasket reduces the compression ratio from 9.1:1 to 8.2:1. There are also minor modifications to the electronic ignition and the fuel injection system.

Output is increased by 35 bhp which means 130 mph and 7.3 0–60 mph time.

Supercharged

A performance option that you might not have considered is supercharging. A supercharger responds immediately, offers excellent boost at low speeds and the power available always matches the demands of the engine. A Scottish company, Fleming Thermodynamics have come up with the Sprintex screw compressor.

Photographs courtesy of Fleming Thermodynamics.

What is it?

The Sprintex consists of two rotors which are placed together in one casing, and mesh without touching. The casing has an inlet and outlet port positioned near the drive.

How does it work?

The larger of the rotors is driven by the engine via a toothed belt, subsequently driving the other through a set of helical gears.

What happens?

(a) The widest space between the rotors occurs at the inlet, which draws air in.
(b) This space is then closed by the end casing.
(c) As the rotors turn the air is forced along and compressed into the outlet port.

The result

Your Vauxhall goes quickly. This application is perfectly suited to the Nova, Astra, and 1.8 Cavalier and Carlton. A 1.3 Nova gets the benefit of the compact Sprintex unit.

VAUXHALL

BODY BUILDING

If you'd like something a bit different there are plenty of body options available. Beauty is obviously in the eye of the beholder, but there's bound to be some addition that makes your Vauxhall just a bit more attractive. Details about the suppliers can be found in the reference section.

Nova
Zenders' Nova with front spoiler, side skirts and alloy wheels.

Astra
The Zender Astra with
integrated spoiler/bumper,
fog lamps, turbo ventilated
light alloy wheels, side
skirts, rear apron and
spoiler.

Cavalier
The Zender approach to the
Cavalier with spoilers, skirts
and alloy wheels.

Carlton
Old and new approaches
by Irmscher.

Senator
Irmscher's front spoiler
with wrap-around bumper
and integrated fog lamps
reduces lift and stability in
cross winds. At the back air
flow is also improved with
the addition of spoiler and
rear apron. They even do
the same for the estate
version.

Droopsnoot

If you can't get hold of the real thing, how about a droop replica? Magard offer a complete panel that fits over the standard Viva. All you have to do is remove grille bumper and lights and then pop rivet the Droop into place. Blend the edges with filler, paint and finally replace the original lights.

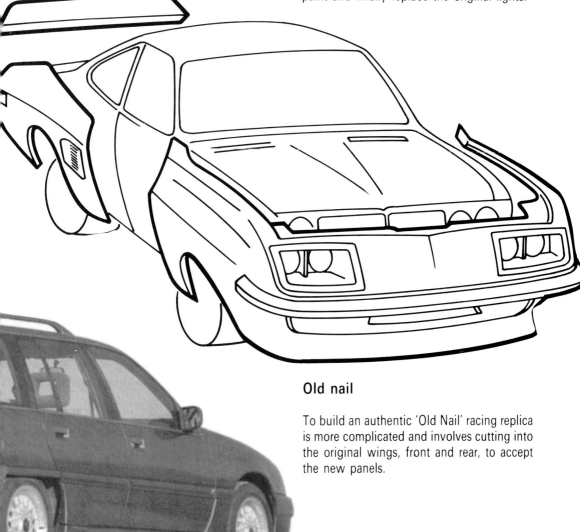

Old nail

To build an authentic 'Old Nail' racing replica is more complicated and involves cutting into the original wings, front and rear, to accept the new panels.

HSR

Want something a little more exciting to do the shopping in? Then a Chevette with a difference would be an HSR clone. Magard have two kits which fit the bill and the car. Either the cost-effective road-going version, or the full rally specification job.

Vauxhall KITS

If merely bolting on some spoilers and skirts is a bit tame for you, why not go the whole hog and take your old Vauxhall to bits! Then you could reassemble it into something that bears virtually no resemblance to a product that once rolled off the Luton or Ellesmere Port production line.

Sylva Leader

Jeremy Phillips has the distinction of being the first kit car manufacturer to utilize Vauxhall parts.

The car was the Sylva Star, first built in 1982 and succeeded by the Leader two years later. The mechanics on both models were Viva HB/HC. Although all sorts of power units could be fitted (including Vauxhall) the suspension has always been standard Viva, which provides excellent handling characteristics.

If the Lotus 7 had been developed beyond the Series 4 then it probably would have ended up looking and performing like the Leader 400.

Leader facts

Body:	Fibreglass
Chassis:	Multi-tubular
Engine:	Vauxhall etc
Transmission:	Viva, or compatible GM unit
Steering:	Viva
Suspension:	Front/Viva (independent, wishbones and coils over shocks)
	Rear/Viva (modified springs with standard dampers)
Wheels:	13–14" or Vauxhall Rostyles
Electrics:	Viva
Contact:	Swindon Sports Cars

Sylva Leader
Andrew Phillips powers a
Sylva leader around
Snetterton in '86

Mumford Musketeer

Is it a bird, plane, squashed insect? No, but it actually started life as a Vauxhall Viva, or in some cases a Chevette. This entertaining 3-wheeler is both fast and economical, thanks to its extremely light construction. The rear wheel powers this little bomb past 80 mph! But you'll still be able to average around 50 mpg. The Musketeer can be bought in various stages of completion.

From the front the glass fibre body suggests that a Ferrari is poised to overtake. Only when it does so can you see the single rear wheel disappearing into the distance!

Musketeer facts

Body:	Glass reinforced polyester resin
Chassis:	Aluminium alloy semi-monocoque
Engine:	Viva HC 1256 cc
Transmission:	HC/Chevette 4-speed
Steering:	Viva rack and pinion
Suspension:	Front/MacPherson strut and coil springs with Spax Gas adjustable inserts. Rear/Swinging arm and coil over shock absorbers
Wheels:	3/Standard Viva
Contact:	Mumford Engineering

Hawk Wyvern

This Wyvern is unusual firstly because it hasn't got four doors, lots of chrome and a body full of rust.

The Hawk Wyvern is an attractive roadster which relies for its mechanics on the Vauxhall Viva. It's available in a cost-effective basic kit that you can finish yourself. A lockable, sturdy construction and of course head-turning style make this a kit worth considering.

Hawk Wyvern facts

Body:	Glass-reinforced polyester resin
Chassis:	Steel
Engine:	Viva HC 1300, or 2.3
Transmission:	HC
Steering:	Viva rack and pinion
Suspension:	Donor Vauxhall
Wheel:	Standard Viva

Coachbuilt

This is not just a casual hacksaw job. These Novas are actually assembled on Irmscher's own production line. The hood is fixed to the top of the windscreen and is stowed between the rear seats and luggage compartment. A hardtop option transforms the Nova into a saloon. All this is achieved without any loss in body strength, or even luggage space! In fact, the Nova has never looked better.

BUYING

By producing reliable, popular and often sporty cars Vauxhall have guaranteed a strong demand for used examples. There is a huge choice, from humble hatchbacks to the luxurious Senators, the Vauxhall range has a car to suit every kind of driver requirement.

The larger saloons offer excellent value for money, although many of the older cars from the '50s and '60s have suffered at the hands of that red peril, rust.

On recent models, a full service history is essential to guarantee that the Vauxhall has been properly maintained. Also a car with a service history will retain its resale value.

Before you buy

Whenever you look at a used Vauxhall, try and take a friend with you to act as an objective eye and ear, ie. to catch things you miss. Never rush a decision, always go away and think about it. Always drive the car and make sure that you look and listen to its performance and appearance. Don't be rushed. If you ever have doubts about any aspect of the car, don't buy it! Believe me there are plenty more Vauxhalls that are just right for you.

The following selection of post-war Vauxhall serves as a general guide to their collectability and general durability with useful tips on what to look for.

The engine

Look where the car has been standing, or move it. Are there oil deposits?

Lift the bonnet and look inside. Examine the engine block as closely as you can; if not weather protected they do crack. Check the radiator and oil level. If any of these fluids have mixed, the cylinder head gasket has probably blown. Start the engine from cold and listen for unwelcome noises from the timing chains, camshafts and tappets. Watch for excessive blue smoke from the exhaust, which can mean that the bores are worn. Once the engine is up to running tem-

perature, with a cloth, remove the oil cap. Smoky fumes will mean that the engine needs a good overhaul.

But being aluminium the unit is more sensitive to abuse, which usually means that the head gasket has failed. Check the fluid levels and the condition of the engine and assess for yourself whether the car has been looked after.

Noisy exhaust? Replacing them is very expensive.

Test drive
Power steering

With the engine running, turn the wheel lock to lock, engine shouldn't falter or stall. Also pump brake, revs should drop slightly. *Automatic transmission*, with engine running apply brake and move gear selector through the D, N and R positions. There should be no audible 'clonks'. With brake stiil applied increase revs when in Drive or Reverse and car should rise at either end. On the road the transmission should respond smoothly. Have a look at the gearbox fluid; if dirty it indicates excessive wear. *On the drive.* Listen for unusual rattles, creaks and knocks. Make sure that you investigate them thoroughly, although it can just be some loose items in the boot. Driving over rough ground will often reveal any suspension weaknesses, such as excessive pitching. *Manuals.* The gear lever should move easily through the gears. There should be no excessive noise in first or reverse gears. Make sure that overdrive, when fitted, will engage. Car should pull away without too much complaint in second.

Looking around

Tyres. Check for wear. If inside tread is worn this is an indication that the suspension is very worn. *Inside.* Make sure that you try out all the 'toys'. If the heater and air conditioning don't work, putting them right can be very expensive. Electric windows must travel smoothly to their full extent, as should the sunroof. Carefully check the condition of the upholstery. Cracked, split or stained leather means an expensive re-trim. The same goes for damaged headlining and badly marked veneer on the dashboard.

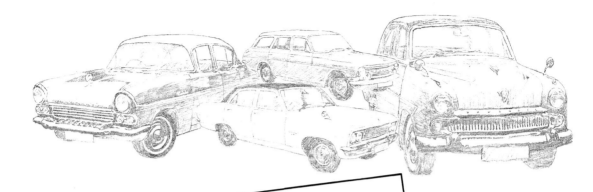

Wyvern, Velox & Cresta

Production history

LIX Wyvern and LIP Velox introduced in 1948. Both cars had identical bodies, although the Velox has bumper overriders and cream wheels. Wyvern powered by 35 bhp 1442 cc engine and the Velox by a 55 bhp 2275 cc unit. This series discontinued in 1951.

For 1951 both models re-styled, now longer, wider and very American, with push button door handles and uprated suspension. From 1952 recirculating ball steering and improved short stroke 1508 cc engine for the Wyvern and a six-cylinder 2262 cc for the Velox. In 1954 restyled bonnet and grille, slimmer pillars (spats over rear wheels for the Velox and Cresta) and wrap around rear windows a year later. Discontinued in 1957 with late improvements such as electric wipers and new grille for Cresta, Velox and Wyvern.

For 1957 the PA six-cylinder cars are completely re-styled. Wheelbase $1\frac{1}{2}$ inches longer, hydraulic clutch and synchromesh gearbox. Cresta more luxurious version. In '58

wrap-around rear windscreen and a year later estate version announced.

Revised 2651 cc engine, grille and larger wheels and tail fins marked the new 1961 models.

The all new PB models in 1962 see the Velox acquiring the 2651 cc engine and the Cresta getting a 3294 cc unit, with servo front disc brakes as standard. From '65 Velox powered by the 3.3 litre engine.

Cresta discontinued in 1965 as larger squarer Cresta PC takes over with more powerful 123 bhp engine. Viscount derivative from 1966 has automatic gearbox, power steering, electric windows, heated rear window, vinyl roof, radio and walnut dashboard as standard. Both models discontinued in 1972.

Mechanics

All Vauxhall units very strong, although look for usual signs of wear. No real weak spots.

Bodywork

Early Vauxhalls rust badly. If the car isn't restored make sure that you look everywhere for rust. Later cars don't have so much of a problem. The original Crestas in particular have the worst reputation. Make sure there's no bodging, i.e. plugging holes with fibreglass and filler.

Spares

Body panels can be a problem: most mechanical items still traceable; membership of the appropriate club is essential to ensure trouble-free running.

Comments & collectability

Early Crestas rare simply because of rust. PAs most popular. Although high prices for nice examples, not expensive to acquire. Remaining Wyverns have no real following. PB and PC ditto. Can get lots of car and rust for your money.

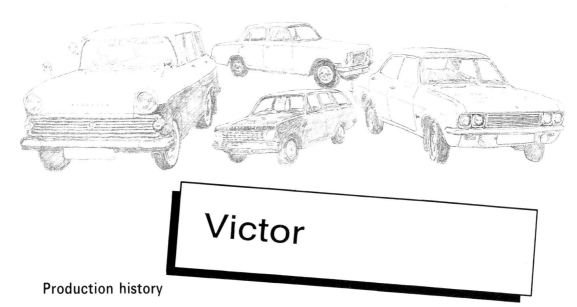

Victor

Production history

F-Type Victor introduced in 1957. The first ever Vauxhall estate is announced a year later. Series 2 car in 1959 has increased bhp output from 48 to 55 bhp, wrap around bumpers and redesigned bonnet with a central rib.

Victor FB in 1961 has a completely new body shape with optional synchromesh gearbox. VX4/90 had twin carburettors and produced 71 bhp. It can be distinguished from less sporty models by its floor gearchange and individual front seats.

Bigger engine, 1595 cc, new dashboard and front disc brakes (not FB) for 1963.

In 1964 another body change, the FC and increased power output 70 bhp and 85 bhp for VX4/90 (which can be identified by its cross-hatch design front grille and colour side strips). Steering column lock is an optional extra and automatic gearbox available from 1966.

FD Victor range introduced in 1967. Has all new body and all new overhead camshaft engine, available as either a 1600 or 2000 cc. Steering now by rack and pinion although disc brakes an option. Renamed Victor Super in 1970 and automatic gearbox available. VX4/90 re-introduced in 1969 has overdrive and Rostyle wheels, overdrive, body coachline and single bar grille. Automatic available for the first time on this model.

From 1968 new luxury derivative the

Ventora and Victor 3300 estate car had a six-cylinder engine producing 123 bhp.

New range of FE Victors from 1972 with restyled bodies. 1800 and 2300 cc engine sizes available. 2.2 litre Ventora II had distinctive "egg box" grille and twin headlamps.

In 1976 Victor name dropped and VX series introduced. VX 1800, 2300 and 2300 GLS (replacing VX4/90) now have revised dashboard, new grille and slimmer bumpers.

Range discontinued in September 1978.

Mechanics
Pushrod engines up until FC in 1967. From FD onward listen for camshaft wear and cylinder head oil leaks. VX4/90s likely to have had harder lives, so make sure gearbox and clutch operating smoothly.

Bodywork

F Victors have worst rust reputation. Later cars not so bad, but always check usual places like wings (inner and outer), sills, doors, boot and floor pan.

Spares

Some panels becoming a problem and as always joining the relevant club helps as new supplies are always being found.

Comments and collectability

F Victor is the best known and most popular, estates very rare. Later FE VX4/90 has a strong following. Low prices though make Victors very affordable and reliable.

Viva, Firenza & Magnum

Production history

Introduced in 1963 as the Viva HA with a 1057 cc engine, rack and pinion steering and synchromesh gearbox. SL model had colour sides and more luxurious trim. Bedford Beagle estate version introduced in 1964. For 1965 sporty HA 90 had a 60 bhp high compression engine and disc brakes.

Re-bodied Viva HB and HB 90 with 2-and 4-door options, revised suspension and 1159 cc engine. Automatic available from 1967 on DL and SL models. High performance Brabham Viva introduced same year with 69 bhp, straight-through exhaust, wider wheels, disc brakes and a Brabham body stripe. In 1968 it was replaced by the Viva GT which had the 2 litre Victor engine, brakes and rear axle. Twin carburettors, close ratio gearbox and 104 bhp make it a genuine sports saloon.

HB 1600 in 1968 has overhead camshaft 1599 cc engine and disc brakes with four doors from '69. HB range discontinued in 1970.

Third generation HC Viva with restyled body (1 inch longer and 1.7 inches wider) which retained 1159 cc engine and 1600 optional on De Luxe and SL models.

For 1971 2-door Coupé called the Firenza is introduced. Top of the range is the 2000 SL. Limited edition Gold Riband HC Viva at the end of '71 with many standard extras such as Rostyle wheels. 1159 units superseded by 1256 in 1972. In the same year Firenza SL introduced with 2300 engine.

In 1973 a luxury Viva called the Magnum available with either 1800 or 2300 engine as 2- and 4-door saloon, estate car and coupé. Distinguished by twin headlamps, side mouldings and Rostyle wheels.

Viva GLS similar to Magnum with twin headlamps, sports wheels and more luxurious interior.

Magnum discontinued in 1977. Viva discontinued 1979.

Mechanics

Generally reliable, though with HB's 1600 (1968) you should always listen for camshaft wear. HA/HB 90 had high compression engines, check for additional modifications and of course signs of abuse. Brakes on HAs never brilliant. 1159 cc and 1256 cc units prone to worn timing chains, disintegrating tappets and sludging in the rocker cover. 1600 cc can suffer from a worn distributor spindle which means a misfire.

Bodywork

HAs are the worst for rust. Sills wings and doors are the most serious areas on all models.

Spares

Apart from HAs body panels no real problem yet. Membership of clubs always helps of course.

Comments & collectability

No Viva sought after apart from real rarities like the Crayford convertible, Brabham Viva HB and the GT. However, practical, reliable and cost-effective transport.

Chevette

Production history

3-door hatchback announced in 1975 with 1256 cc engine. 'E' economy version in basic trim has limited production run.

Following year hatchback joined by 2- and 4-door saloons as well as a 2-door estate version. E has no reclining seats, L has bright window surrounds, plaid trim, GLS has chrome bumper lower grille, sill and wheelarches, sports wheels, velour trim, centre console and clock. Automatic option on L and GL also in '79. Re-style this year with flush headlamps.

Range continues basically unchanged with

better equipped limited editions, Command Performance 3-door '80, Black Pearl '81, Silhouette '82, whilst phasing out models from 1982. Chevette officially discontinued in 1984.

Mechanics

Mainly used as 'shopping' car so make sure that clutch and gearbox are working smoothly. Stop-start motoring may have led to premature wear on the engine.

Bodywork

Rust on wings, sills, doors and tailgate.

Spares

No problems.

Comments & collectability

No Chevette with the exception of the HS (which counts as a Droop Snoot anyway) is in demand. Cheap and reliable.

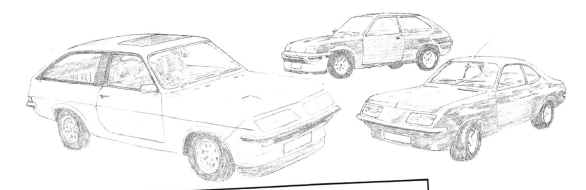

Droop Snoots

Production history

High performance Firenza 'droop snoot' coupé in 1974. 2.3 litre engine with high lift camshaft and Stromberg carburettors with 5-speed ZF gearbox. Bodywork and trim consisted of fibreglass nose, alloy wheels (185/70 tyres), rear spoiler, special paint (silver with matt black window surrounds) and trim. Sports Hatch, basically estate Firenza with coupé body modifications and finish.

In March '78 limited edition 2300HS

hatchback had 16 valve, twin cam engine giving 135 bhp with front/rear spoiler. Available to special order only from 1979.

1980 HSR with 150 bhp engine plus glassfibre bonnet and side skirts.

Mechanics

Firenza engine very strong, so just look out for signs of wear or neglect. Main bearing on the crankshaft can go and valves burn out. Cambelts should be changed every 35,000 miles and could sound squeaky. Two-piece propshaft can cause problems and many owners swop to one-piece.

Bodywork

Rust can attack the front wings, wheel arches, doors, sills, inner wing and windscreen pillars. Check for accident damage. Chevette HS (sb).

Spares

Genuine nosecones available from the Droop Snoot Group who are an excellent source for all parts. Droop Snoot wings no longer available but existing Viva HC wings can be modified. Coupé doors difficult to find. Chevette has good parts availability.

Comments & collectability

As only 200 Coupés, 200 Sportshatches, 400 HRs and 50 HSRs built, very rare cars. However, prices are presently very low for Droop Snoots, a neglected car, but this can't last for long.

Membership of the Droop Snoot Group is essential.

Cavalier

Production history

2- and 4-door saloon announced in 1975 with 1584 or 1897 cc (Coupé has 1897) engine. Basic L model, GL has side moulding, bright metal trim on sill and wheelarches, velour cloth trim and clock. Coupé GL has front spoiler, four spoke steering wheel and wood finish door inserts. Automatic is optional across range.

1977 1300 saloon introduced with no automatic option. The following year Sports hatchback 1600 GLS introduced and along with 2000 GLS offered with hatchback. Two-door coupé discontinued the following year.

Second generation front wheel drive Cavalier introduced in August '81 as 1.3, or 1.6 4-door saloon and 5-door hatchback. Body is totally redesigned. Automatic is an option. Opel Manta takes over from the sports hatchback.

1800 injection models follow the next year (along with 1600 diesel option). SRi has alloy

wheels, two tone paint, tinted glass and Recaro seats. CD has brown bumpers, front spoiler, electric front windows and power steering. New Manta has front spoiler, side mouldings, colour keyed bumpers. Convertible introduced in 1985. CD discontinued in 1986 GLi, GLSi remain with new engines. New model the 2000i has electric windows, rear head restraints, alloy wheels and power steering.

Sep '87 Manta Berlinetta discontinued, GT gets halogen headlamps and leather steering wheel. Nov '87 LX models with alloy wheels, glass sunroof and sports seats for 1600 and 1800 Cavaliers.

Replaced by new model in September 1988.

Mechanics

Most common signs of wear, especially if used as a company car, include rattling camshaft and knocking bearings. The gear-box can also give trouble with synchromesh wearing out on second. Early cars also drank oil because of inadequate valve stem oil seals. As for handling make sure that the steering doesn't pull the car to one side, ditto brakes. Fuel injection versions trouble-free but not easy DIY.

Bodywork

Be on the look out for accident repair, i.e. misaligned panels and overspray. Rust can attack the inner wings, wheel arches and sills.

Spares

No problems.

Comments & collectability

As favoured by fleet users make sure that the mileage is genuine, i.e. does the condition of the car tally with the odometer reading? Hatchbacks sell for more than saloons.

Carlton, Royale, Viceroy & Senator

Production history

New large saloon and estates introduced in 1978, Carlton with 1800 and 2000 engines and more luxurious six-cylinder front wheel drive Royale with saloon and hatchback coupé bodies. Royale has electric windows, tinted glass, automatic transmission and power steering as standard.

Viceroy in 1980 2.5 litre version of the

Royale, discontinued along with the Royale in '82. In same year Carlton diesel announced.

Carlton CD in '83 has injected engine, electric windows, sliding roof, alloy wheels and rear head restraints. Replaced by 2200i in 1984.

Also in '84 Opel Senator rebadged as a Vauxhall with 2.5 and 3.0 litre engines. Sunroof, power steering and central locking standard. In addition the 3.0 has auto gearbox, electric windows and head restraints included. CDi had air conditioning, trip computer and electric roof.

New restyled Carlton introduced in 1986. 1.8L and 1.8iL with power steering, split rear seat and speaker system are standard. GL has sunroof, headlamp wash/wipe, electric door mirrors and sunroof. CD has alloy wheels, electric windows, cruise control and luxurious interior. 2.0i has same specifications for GL and CD. 3.0i GSi follows in March '87, specifications as CD plus cruise control, rear suspension levelling, ABS, sports seats, leather trim and trip computer.

New 3.0i Senator in September 1987, as Carlton GSi plus electric ride control and six speaker stereo.

Mechanics

Check for wear on camshaft and big ends. Check that power steering functioning correctly and that no noises or stalling occur when turned from lock to lock.

Bodywork

No real rust problems, just look along sills and for stone chips that have turned to rust.

Spares

No problems.

Comments & collectability

A lot of car for your money. Coupé is neglected performer. Make sure that all the extras work. Only problem is that the 3.0 units do gobble petrol.

Nova

Production history

New small Vauxhall introduced in April 1983 and available with 1, 1.2, or 1.3 litre engine in a 2-door saloon hatchback body. 1.3 SR has spoilers, side mouldings, sports wheels, sports seats, extra instruments and tinted glass.

From 1985 5-door 1.2 and 1.3 Novas are offered. Also Merit special edition with rear

wash/wipe, side striping, head restraints, quartz clock and tweed trim, retained as production model throughout range.

Mechanics

Excessive engine noise and smoke not uncommon if used around town, along with clutch and gearbox wear. Steering with a mind of its own means that the wheels have been kerbed once too often.

Bodywork

No problems, particularly because of 6 year anti-corrosion warranty, apart from stone chips turning to rust.

Spares

No problems.

Comments & collectability

Very popular on the used car market and sporty SR and GTE versions have broadened the appeal and could be future 'classics.' Cheap to run and maintain.

Astra / Belmont

Production history

All new Astra range, Vauxhall version of German Opel Kadett. Front wheel drive with 1200, or 1300 cc units with 3-door, 5-door and estate options. A year later 1600 cc engine becomes available and diesel variant in '82.

Sporty 3-door GTE in 1983, front/rear spoilers, wheel arch/sill extension, Recaro seats, 5-speed gearbox and tinted glass.

In October '84 new shape Astra introduced with same engine sizes. L has radio cassette, clock and split rear seats. GL has front head restraints, adjustable steering column and tinted windows. SR has sports seats, headlamp washers and spoilers. GTE is discontinued in '85, SRi takes its place. GTE

re-introduced in September 1987 with 2.0 engine. Convertible also available.

New Vauxhall saloon introduced in January 1986 (known as the Belmont, with 1300, 1600 (automatic option and 1600 diesel) and fuel injected 1800, the GLSi. By end of year 1.3 and 1.6 engines revised and automatic option on GLSi which now has head restraints and electric windows.

January '87 SRi introduced with sports seats headlamp washers, tinted windows, plaid cloth trim and fleece carpets.

Mechanics

Early 1.3 units had oil starvation that meant camshaft wear and failure of valve stem seals too didn't help. Otherwise units strong and can go beyond 60,000 miles without major overhaul. Still check for wear though.

Bodywork

On the older shape just look for rust in the usual places, wings, sills and tailgate and stone chips around the front of the car.

Spares

No problems.

Comments & collectability

Interior can become scruffy on higher mileage cars. 1.3 or 1.6 are probably the best engines to go for. GTEs will probably be viewed in the future as a desirable hot hatchback.

VAUXHALL TODAY

The late seventies were not particularly happy times for Vauxhall. Constantly in the red, many regarded the range, particularly at the lower end, as rather dull and long in the tooth.

One of the most significant moves was to clear up the public confusion between Opels and Vauxhalls, especially as GM product rationalisation meant that only the badges and prices were different. So the cars became either Vauxhalls or Opels, but never both. And with the dealer network integrated, all they needed was a sales-winning product range.

Astra

1979: A Viva replacement, but a very different car. Originally imported from Germany, where it is known as the Kadett, production was started at Ellesmere Port. Offering 5-door flexibility with a range of 1200, 1300 and 1600 cc engines it spearheaded the Vauxhall revival. The sporty GTE also broadened the model's appeal.

1984: Perhaps the most surprising move was to totally re-design the car even before the shape had dated. This aerodynamic treatment

was to set the style for all '80s and '90s Vauxhalls.

1986: The Belmont is the booted addition to the family.

Nova

1983: Vauxhall's entry into the supermini class was relatively late. But it has since proved to be one of Britain's most popular 'shopping' cars in both 2- and 3-door forms.

1985: The addition of 4- and 5-door models complete the line-up.

Cavalier

1982: The Cavalier was a popular car throughout the '70s, but when the revamp came the model literally took off. Rapidly the saloon and hatchbacks pushed Vauxhall to the top of the sales charts. Front wheel drive, a new body and traditional reliability made it a firm favourite with the British public. Fleet Car of the Year 1985, 1986 and 1987.

1988: Again Vauxhall took the market lead in the saloon class. Low drag design, more room, and advanced suspension are just

some of the improvements. Exciting new developments include the 16 valve engine and 4 wheel drive.

Carlton

1982: Facelift re-established the Carlton as one of the best executive saloons.
1986: All new model reflected the Vauxhall aerodynamic approach to design. Engine sizes include 1800 cc, 2.0i, 2.3 diesel and 3.0i. The GSi with body kit, ABS and leather trim offer the combination of power with comfort that only German cars have offered in the past. 1987 Car of the Year.

Senator

1984: Introduced as Vauxhall after Opel badging. First luxury Vauxhall for many years available with 2.5 or 3.0 litre power.
1987: New shape with distinctive egg-box grille. Comprehensive equipment list on the 3.0 litre make this the perfect up-market package.

This completes one of the most up-to-date ranges in Europe.

Manufacturing facts

Luton

Employees:	6,000
Car plant staff:	4,000
Cars per hour:	30
Output per year:	94,000
Exported:	4,500
Technology:	£90 million paint plant

VAUXHALL ADVERTISING

Ellesmere Port

Employees:	5,000
Output per year:	114,000
Vehicle:	Astras, Belmonts and Astra Vans
Investment:	£100 million since '84
Technology:	£50 million computer-controlled robot production line.

Over the last few years Vauxhall's advertising has been amongst some of the most distinctive and memorable promotions for motor cars. Which is what it's all about of course.

Here's a selection of cheeky ads from Vauxhall's agency, Lowe Howard Spink. Could they be getting at their rivals perhaps?

Conclusive proof that the Astra could house the obedience section at Crufts if need be. Although as the ad explains, they were aiming for 16, but a last minute difference of opinion between a Tibetan mastiff and long-coated chihuahua put paid to that.

YOU CAN NOW GET FOURTEEN ROVERS IN THE BACK OF A VAUXHALL ASTRA.

Actually, we were aiming for sixteen.

Only there was a last minute difference of opinion between a Tibetan mastiff and a long-coated chihuahua.

Nevertheless, we think the point is made.

The carrying capacity of the new Astra Estate is quite remarkable for its size.

Just for the record (and it is a record), that extra-wide tailgate opens on to 53.7 cubic feet of usable space.

The smooth, uncluttered floor area is nearly 4' longer than our nearest rival's.

And the payload of half a ton would make many estates throw up their front wheels in complete horror.

Rest assured, the Astra's uncanny resemblance to a warehouse vanishes at the turn of an ignition key.

The choice of 1.3, 1.6 or 1.6-diesel engines all whisk the car from 0-60 mph before you can say Jack Russell.

The sleek drag co-efficient of just 0.35 results in some pretty extraordinary fuel economy figures.

Whilst the well-appointed interior shares the same high trim and equipment levels as its hatchback counterpart.

All this and half of Cruft's to boot?

Perhaps it's time for a quick walkies down to your local Vauxhall-Opel dealer.

THE NEW VAUXHALL ASTRA ESTATE.

Remember, we got here first.

THE ENGINE IS SO QUIET YOU CAN ALMOST HEAR THE COMPUTER TALKING TO IT.

It's uncanny.

Turn the key in the new Senator CD and all you hear is a faint, far off hum.

The hushed tone continues as you engage drive and pull effortlessly away.

Even at speed, peace prevails.

There's no shriek from the engine, no whine from the wind, no roar from the road.

Clearly this is a car of exceptional refinement. The top of the Vauxhall range, no less.

The 3.0i six cylinder engine has years of progressive development behind it.

With hydraulic tappets and 12 crankshaft counterweights, it's a very smooth engine indeed. ('Smooth as a baby's bottom' as one review put it.)

To further dowse the decibels, we increased the size of the silencer and fitted a sound-absorbing lining to the bonnet.

And to create a thoroughly civilised car all-round, we built in computers, ten of them in all.

The Bosch L2 management system and the AT4CC automatic transmission system are on particularly good terms.

Between them they smooth each and every gearchange.

First, the AT4CC warns the Bosch L2 that a gearchange is imminent.

Then the Bosch L2 tells the engine to reduce the revs momentarily to allow a seamless, surge-free gearchange.

"The transmission helps the impression of great refinement. Even kickdowns are achieved with little more sign than a slurred change of engine note" said Autocar.

Motor agreed: "Smooth the gearchanges are – comparable with the best".

And, we might add, the gears boast a feature found on no other car in this class.

'Winter', 'Economy' and 'Power' settings.

'Winter' bypasses first and second gears to give the improved traction of a start in third on snow and ice.

In 'Economy' the transmission changes normally, while in 'Power' it shifts at higher revs for peak performance.

Needless to say, the AT4CC monitors every move.

Meanwhile other computers are busying themselves elsewhere.

Assisting the power-assisted steering for instance.

Varying the power according to your speed so you never lose touch with the road.

Another computer allows you to adjust the suspension and choose from three different ride settings, 'Comfort', 'Medium' and 'Sports'.

While the seven-function trip computer lets you call up information such as your average speed, average fuel consumption or the temperature outside.

It will even tell you how far you can go on the remaining fuel.

The Senator Factfile will tell you the rest of the Senator story.

For a copy, call 0800 400 462.

You'll discover how the ABS brakes, the cruise control, the electric windows and the heating system all make use of microprocessors.

To make the Senator CD relaxing, not taxing, to drive.

THE SENATOR CD.

VAUXHALL. ONCE DRIVEN, FOREVER SMITTEN.

Above: If you thought the quietest car in the world had a scantily clad lady perched precariously atop the radiator, a Griffin would almost certainly disagree. The advanced computer technology which keeps a Senator moving smoothly obviously makes a difference. *Below:* Any doubts about what is the safest estate on the road? The defection of some rather well known characters makes the point. A rigid steel safety cage, crumple zones, child proof locks and anti-jamming doors all add up to an incredibly protective package. The Carlton Estate, obviously chosen by the more intelligent dummies.

MORE AND MORE FAMILIES ARE SWITCHING TO THE CARLTON ESTATE.

Think of an estate car and you'll most probably think of a Volvo. Quite honestly, it would be difficult not to.

Over the years you've heard more about its considerable virtues than just about any other estate car.

And why not.

The Volvo's safety record is there for everyone to see.

Now however, we at Vauxhall have a car that even the Swedes will have to sit up and take notice of.

The Carlton Estate.

A car that not only looks after you when you're in trouble, but helps you avoid it in the first place.

Our confidence in the Carlton is based upon something no other car has. 'Advanced Chassis Technology' or ACT.

ACT is a suspension system so sophisticated you won't even know it's there.

Until you need it.

In an emergency, the system will help stabilise your car to prevent possible fishtailing and spinning.

Brake suddenly and ACT will help bring your car to a controlled and straight halt, whether the road is wet or dry.

Hopefully you'll never have to put it to the test. Unlike Autocar magazine that is, who described its degree of stability as "truly remarkable".

But if it does come to the crunch the Carlton will leap straight to your defence.

A rigid steel safety cage, front and rear crumple zones, child-proof locks, anti-jamming doors. Our safety specifications are the equal of anyone's.

The Carlton also boasts fuel economy that other estates can only envy and a maximum load capacity most cars would choke on (a massive 65.3 cu ft. no less).

Hardly surprising then that in 1987 the Carlton was voted Car of the Year.

More importantly, Motor magazine concluded in a comparative test report with the Volvo 740GLE that the Carlton was "most certainly the better estate car".

Their words, not ours.

For further information please call 0800-400-462.

THE CARLTON ESTATE.

VAUXHALL. ONCE DRIVEN, FOREVER SMITTEN.

9 OUT OF 10 CATS PREFER CARLTONS.

It's late. You've had a rotten day and can't wait to get home.

You hang a left then change up into 3rd.

Suddenly, from nowhere, something runs out in front of you. (This time it's a cat. But it could easily have been a small child.)

What do you do? In some cars, you could be in trouble.

Swerve and you run the risk of fishtailing or spinning. Slam on the brakes and you could well veer off the road or worse, into on-coming traffic.

Your only option then is to pray.

At Vauxhall, we know only too well that situations like this happen all to often.

Heaven forbid it should happen to you. But if it does, your prayers would have more chance of being answered driving a Carlton Estate.

Our faith in the Carlton is based upon something no other car has. We call it 'Advanced Chassis Technology', or A.C.T.

ACT is a system designed to work hardest when you really need it.

In an emergency, it will help bring your car to a controlled and straight halt.

Should you need to swerve, the system will help to stabilise your car, which in turn will help you to stay in control.

When Autocar put it to the test they simply described it as 'truly remarkable'.

However, our concern for safety doesn't just stop there.

A rigid steel safety cage, front and rear crumple zones, child-proof locks, anti-jamming doors. Our safety specifications are the equal of anyone's.

The Carlton also boasts fuel economy that other estates can only envy and a maximum load capacity most cars would choke on (a massive 65.3 cu. ft. no less.)

Hardly surprising then that in

1987 the Carlton was voted Car of the Year.

More importantly, Motor magazine concluded in a comparative test report with the Volvo 740 GLE that the Carlton was "most certainly the better estate car".

Their words, not ours.

For further information phone 0800 400 462.

THE CARLTON ESTATE.

VAUXHALL. ONCE DRIVEN, FOREVER SMITTEN.

Quite simply, if you're an animal lover, you really shouldn't be driving anything else. ACT, or Advanced Chassis Technology, gives you more control and stability when taking kitty avoidance measures. But what about hedgehogs? The Vauxhall boffins are probably working on that now.

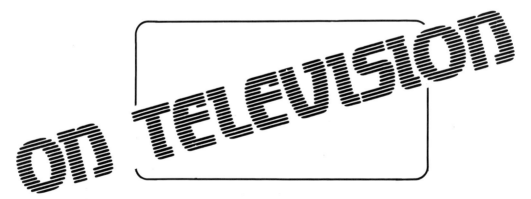

If the Red Arrows were ever grounded they'd probably get airborne again behind the wheel of an Astra. Certainly one of the most striking ads ever produced, there were no trick camara angles, all the stunts were genuine.

When some people go for a test drive, they really go for a test drive. Because in an Astra they're likely to win the odd international rally. Then cruise through the South of France and ascend the Alps in a Carlton for an important rendezvous. But at least they end up taking most of the showroom with them.

A Cavalier LX is driven effortlessly along an empty country road. It then pulls into a lay-by so that we can appreciate the excellent spec' of metallic paint, alloy wheels etc. The driver makes a phone call to his wife to moan about the traffic conditions. Martin Shaw looks particularly pleased with himself. Cavalier and Shaw drive off into the sunset accompanied by the tune 'Layla' and the line "Once Driven Forever Smitten"

Conclusion? Either a Cavalier helps you recapture your youth, or turns you into a compulsive liar.

Cavalier campaign

This was the most expensive and extensive car launch ever which swallowed up £10 million in just two months. But at least everyone was talking about the new Cavalier.

The host of a '50s TV programme invites us to watch 'Step into the future.' Poster sites all over the country also put out the same message. A small boy watches in awe as this Motor Car of Tomorrow is unveiled. 30 years later he finally gets his hands on that car, in the shape of the Cavalier.

In supplements and motor magazines the '50s theme is continued in comic book style.

Opening up the gatefold flaps reveals the 'real' Cavalier ads underneath.

An impressive series of colour plates photographed by Andrew Yeadon graced the pages of the motoring press.

Campaign Facts: More than 3,500 Poster sites. Keith Watson, an artist on the original Dan Dare Comics, drew the magazine spreads. Bob Danvers-Walker from Take your Pick was used for the radio ads.

Building a Vauxhall

It takes millions of pounds' worth of equipment, more than 14,000 individual parts, quality control inspectors and many assembly line workers to build your new Vauxhall. But how do they combine to put it all together?

1. Press shop

(a) High quality sheet and coil steel is delivered by road.

(b) Cut to the required length by automatic guillotines.

(c) Then passed along a line of six presses to produce the panels.

2. Sub-assembly

(a) Pressings are joined by multi-weld machines to make the frame for the engine-transmission and the front and rear sub-assemblies.

(b) These are then robot-welded to make up the underbody which is then transferred to the body framing line.

(c) The doors and body sides go through their own welding process which includes hemming and heating in ovens to set the panel adhesive.

3. Body building

The sub-assemblies are welded together by a combination of man and robot working together to form the complete body. Quality checks make sure that everything is correctly aligned. With the doors, wings, bonnet and tailgate, or boot, in place the frame is now known as the 'body in white'.

4. Paint

Vauxhalls are subject to an extensive 10 stage paint process. But before any colour is applied the body itself is fully prepared.

Many parts are zinc plated (doors, windscreen pillars, bonnet).

Epoxy-based adhesive-sealant to prevent moisture being trapped.

Washing body in alkali and hot water.

The 10 stage process. 1. Phosphate applied 2. Oven dried and then 3. Rinsed in chromic acid 4. Dipped in primer 5. Electrostatically applied primer 6. Sanding 7. Washing and 8. Sealer coat then finally 9. Acrylic lacquer paint which gives it colour. 10. Colour baked on.

In addition, sills and inner panels are waxed for extra protection.

5. Trim

After painting, the doors are removed and trimmed away from the production line. The dashboards are also assembled in this way. The painted shells are fitted with seats, carpets and headlining.

6. Final assembly

A marriage conveyor system raises the body above ground level whilst trucks carrying the engine and transmission run below. Jacks raise the mechanics to meet the underbody. As the body returns to the factory floor the wheels are balanced then fitted. The essential fluids, coolant, petrol and oil are added. The original doors are returned to the body.

7. Finish

The car is now driven through a series of checking stations. Headlight beam is set. Wheels aligned. Exhaust emissions are measured on the rolling road. A water test checks the sealing around the doors, windows and boot/tailgate. Paintwork blemishes are rectified, the car is washed, valeted and badged. Engine and underbody waxing, the brakes are checked. Finally the new Vauxhall is driven from the production line.

True Stories

Far-fetched, occasionally tall, mostly amusing, sometimes there are witnesses, often just a rumour and sometimes a little truth. But what all these tales have in common though, is a Vauxhall in some shape, or form. I hope you enjoy them.

If you were offered a low mileage, excellent condition, one owner Nova for just a few hundred pounds, wouldn't you jump at the chance? Well that's exactly what Roger Phillips did when he was on the look out for a little Vauxhall runabout.

His wife June had said that she liked the look of the Vauxhall Nova and Roger was determined to find one that they could both share. It would make life so much easier, dropping the children to school then both going on to work. The only problem would be the money, they didn't have a lot of it. However, as well as closely reading all the local papers Roger made sure that all his friends knew what he wanted.

About a week after starting the search, he got a call from a car dealer who said that he had a Nova for Roger at just the right price. The only catch was that the dealer needed a decision over the phone because the car was taking up too much space on the forecourt. The special offer price was just £250. But Roger wanted to make sure that he would get value for money. "What's it like?" he asked innocently. "All the usual extras" came the reply. These included power steering, air conditioning, electric windows, electric door mirrors, electric aerial, metallic paint, white wall tyres etc.

It sounded too good to be true yet Roger was willing to take a chance. Before he left for work the next day he gave June an envelope containing the cash and said that a man would be delivering something later on

in the day.

To say that June got the shock of her life is a slight understatement. And when Roger returned home he wondered what a huge American car was doing outside his house, and apparently blocking out most of the available sunlight. Roger had been the victim of Chinese whispers. As his friends had asked other friends to look out for a Vauxhall Nova, it had become abbreviated to Nova and mentioned to an American car dealer who had an appropriately cheap Chevrolet Nova.

The car concerned was a 1972 2-door with a huge V8 engine, although it was at least a General Motors product. For its age it was in very good condition and all the electric toys worked. The Phillips' had no complaints apart from the fuel bills, parking problems and higher insurance. Luckily they were accosted by an American car freak in Tesco's car park who needed a Nova to add to his collection. You can guess what they bought with the proceeds from the Chevrolet. That's right, a hatchback Nova of the Vauxhall variety.

It was a relatively quiet war for private Bertie Harris. But in the tank regiment he managed to pick up a lot of skills as well as a Vauxhall 10 car!

Bertie's main concerns were keeping the staff car fleets running, as well as anything else that was supposed to move. The name of the game in the army at that time was cannibalize. This meant that if you had two vehicles that didn't work, you really should be able to get one that does out of them, and as new replacement parts were almost impossible to come by, this was vital.

However, out of the cannibalized parts there was always something that seemed to get left over. Harris reckoned that it was a shame to leave items such as gearlevers, headlights and seats to accumulate dust on the spares shelf.

On the waste not, want not principle Bertie decided to send certain parts home once it was clear that they weren't going to be used. Once they arrived at his East London home, car-mad younger brother Joe would then be able to assemble it piece by piece. Hopefully by the time he went home for good there would be a Vauxhall 10 waiting for him.

Surprisingly, Bertie encountered very few problems in the mail order car business, although there was one occasion when he almost got caught and court-martialled.

Body panels were always a problem to send off and the offside door was no exception. He wrapped it in brown paper with added newspaper for protection. Everything was then tied up with string. The few yards to the despatch office were always worrying, but Harris always made sure that the NCOs were enjoying themselves in the mess. But coming out of the office as he was going in was Staff Sergeant Hardy. "Where are yew taking that parcil 'arris?" he asked in his usual blunt manner, "an wot the 'ell is in there?"

Harris froze, but reasoned that honesty was probably the best policy. "I'm posting the offside door of a Vauxhall home to me brother." The Sergeant narrowed his eyes, smiled, opened his mouth and laughed, chuckling as he marched away.

And that was the closest he came to getting caught out. When Bertie finally made it home in 1947 the Vauxhall, save for a few bits of Humber and Ford, was complete. The 10 lasted until '63 when one of the new-fangled Vivas took its place.

The *Vauxhall Motorist* magazine during the '30s introduced a character to their readers called Pamela. Each issue's story always involved Pamela and a Vauxhall.

Adventure tales, romantic stories and light hearted romps, whatever the outcome, Pamela always drove into the sunset at the wheel of her faithfull Vauxhall.

" . . . sobbing her heart out against the waterproof coat."

Recently several major record companies decided to find out just what the nation's drivers were listening to. That way they'd know which records to make more of. A large market research campaign was mounted and aimed at specific driving groups. Lorry drivers, taxi drivers, chauffeurs etc.

However, when it came to reps, perhaps the largest group of professional drivers, it was decided to interview the owners of just one make of car. And what else would a representative be driving but a Cavalier?

Most of the questionnaires were answered at motorway service areas and the results were as follows: *Best female singer*: Sade, *Best male singer*: Sting, *Best group*: Dire Straits, *Best classical*: Mozart, *Best comedy*: Tony Hancock, *Least played*: Des O'Connor.

For a car to be given the nickname "the lemming", there's either something very wrong with the motor itself, or the driver is 'a piston short of a block'. In this case, the poor, battered little Viva was most definitely the innocent party.

Arthur Wendle never pretended that he was anything more than a very average driver and over the years of Viva ownership, he did nothing to suggest otherwise. But on one occasion, Arthur managed to turn a pleasant family outing into an international incident.

One of the more pleasant features of visiting the seaside is that you can park your car on the promenade and sit a few yards away on the beach. The Wendles did this at Weston-Super-Mare. But Arthur's failure to apply the handbrake, combined with a slight incline and a gust of wind meant that the Viva soon joined them on the beach. The car also

brought one hamburger stand and a pile of deck chairs with it. As luck would have it, these objects only fractionally missed a party from the Belgian Consulate who were relaxing below. However, the Viva ended up nose down in the sand whilst the deck chairs showered a coach party from Bristol and the hamburgers brought every dog in the area running.

Over the following years there were a number of further scrapes with the Wendle Viva, one of which included a failure to stop far enough away from the back of a police panda car. Thump! All of this did nothing for

Arthur's insurance premium. But still it didn't persuade him to gracefully retire from motoring.

The latest near-fatal incident involved Arthur, the HB Viva and a multi-storey car park. Leaving your car in reverse after parking it, isn't particulary clever, especially if you plan on re-starting it without first changing to neutral. And if you do that six storeys up, you're not likely to live to tell the tale, unless of course your name is Arthur Wendle. He managed to take his foot off the accelerator in time, but the badly damaged boot was still left dangling dangerously over the street below.

The Viva might be called "Lemming", but I think the owner ranks as a right "lemon".

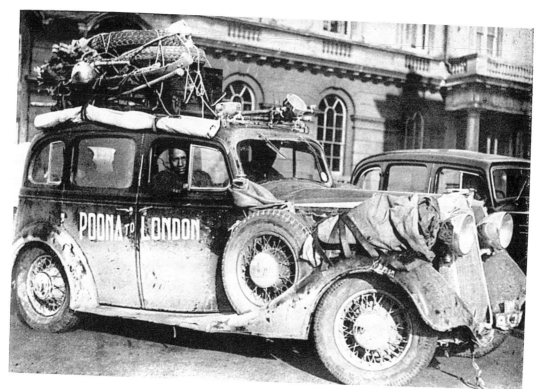

Mr. Khasgiwale travelled from Poona to London in the astonishingly short time of 29 days 8 hours. These days it takes that long to complete a circuit of the M25. He did this at the wheel of a Vauxhall.

There were many scrapes and misunderstandings at several border posts along the way that nearly resulted in arrest. Finding petrol occasionally proved a problem, but he finally arrived safely with the Vauxhall in one piece, in a record time that has yet to be beaten.

Successful attempts on this record will obviously find themselves included in *The Vauxhall Driver's Book II*.

Emily Donaldson was careful with her money, which is another way of saying that she was terribly mean, and like most mean people she didn't trust anyone else with money, least of all banks.

But she didn't resort to making her lumpy mattress even lumpier Emily knew that there was one unit of exchange that was negotiable the world over and even increased in value. It was the perfect investment, gold.

Every penny of her not inconsiderable savings was converted into sovereigns. What happened to these sovereigns was a mystery. Her greedy children on their infrequent visits always made sure that they rummaged around the house, but always failed to find the gold haul.

When old Emily finally popped off, her offspring were not surprisingly rather interested in the contents of her will. Everything was divided equally, but there was no mention of the gold. The four children then moved into the house and proceeded to pull it apart. But JCBs in the garden and chainsaws through the floorboards refused to yield any buried treasure. So the house and its contents were sold off.

Car enthusiast Robert Hanley managed to acquire the engineless Vauxhall Victor from Emily's garage for £150. That was by no means a bargain, but Robert was pleased to see that many of the panels were virtually rust free, something almost unheard of on a 1957 vintage Victor.

Once it had been towed home, Robert set about removing the hand painted layers of paint. And as the paint stripper took effect it wasn't the steel surface that shone through.

What Emily had done was melt the sovereigns down in the kitchen and then carefully pour the molten contents onto the body panels. Once it had set, she painted over the bodywork with any old paint, that happened to be lying around. Her flawless reasoning was: who could possibly steal one without an engine from within a barricaded garage?

And was the Victor worth its weight in gold? Almost. £15,000 was the approximate value and legally Emily's greedy kids couldn't claim a single panel!

How far will Luton enthusiasts go to surround themselves with all things Vauxhall? Edmund Lindsay, events Organiser for the Droop Snoot group has named his house Vauxholme. Geddit?

In fact the Lindsay Brothers, Edmund and Mario must rate as the most committed Vauxhall enthusiasts in the world. It all started because their father's haulage firm always ran Bedfords and Vauxhalls, and when they noticed that Bill Blydenstein and Gerry Marshall had started to race Vivas they had found their heroes.

Over the following years they wrote to everyone who had anything to do with Vauxhalls and regularly received postal vans full of replies. After acquiring literally tons of posters, magazines, brochures and models they eventually got hold of the real thing in the shape of a Viva estate. However, their real love has always been the Droop Snoots and several years later they ran a pair of Chevette HSs.

The practical demands of the haulage business meant they swopped those cars for Cavaliers, although they bought a Droop between them. Several interesting cars later they rescued Silver Bullet, Wayne Cherry's concept car, from the roof of the Luton Design studio. Today it has been restored to its former glory.

And as for their fleet of Bedfords, although the Griffin has long disappeared from production models, the Lindsays make sure that those little red symbols take pride of place on their lorries.

I think that makes them the biggest Vauxhall fans of all time, unless someone else knows better . . .

. . . Well perhaps Miriam Carroll who works in Vauxhall's Public Affairs office does. She vividly remembers receiving a facinating picture from some Luton enthusiasts 'down under.' As well as owning Vauxhall's they also sought to indoctrinate the youngest members of their family. Emblazoned on every one of the baby's nappies was a friendly Luton Griffin!

'Floppy disc' usually refers to a single record made of a particularly thin vinyl. But take away the 'py' and you've got a 'flop'. This record is both.

Amateur singer Bernard Hartley saw the perfect opportunity to exploit the popularity

est Viva My Viva

of a holiday song and a very successful car made in Luton. 'Est Viva my Viva' was recorded in half an hour with the Sid Raven trio and issued on cost-effective thin vinyl.

The idea was to promote and sell the record during his night club appearances, get a cult following and then secure a proper record deal. That was the plan, but sadly for Bernard it didn't work. 350 records are still flopping around his Viva's boot.

When the Rose family returned from their caravan holiday in Cornwall it was a pretty uneventful journey back to Long Eaton in Derbyshire. However, there was a rather annoying squeak coming from somewhere in their Cavalier.

As soon as they arrived home Dave Rose got underneath the Cavalier and started to dismantle the suspension. At first it looked to Dave as though a bit of old carpet had got stuck in the spring, but as he tugged at it, the carpet moved!

It turned out to be a very tired and dirty hedgehog. Although shaken after its 300 mile ordeal 'Henry', as he was soon christened, reacted well to the cat food and saucer of milk offered by Mrs. Rose as refreshment. Henry was passed into the capable hands of the RSPCA who later released him into the Derbyshire countryside.

The theory is that Henry huddled up inside the Cavalier's coil spring for warmth (well it was a British summer) and was not surprisingly too frightened to jump out once the car started moving. Perhaps it also proves that hedgehogs know that Vauxhall Cavalier owners are going to look after them!

One advantage of having a GM car is that many of the parts are interchangeable. Breakdown in Europe and you'll get a Kadett part that will fit your Astra, or Omega for your Carlton etc . . . Appropriately Opel Vauxhall club member Henry Jones has converted his Vauxhall Nova into an Opel Corsa. Carefully replacing all the bits and bobs, from badges to horn buttons, with things that say Opel. The only question is why? I suppose because it was there.

In 1969 a Ventora was stolen from the Colliver Fisher Garage and involved in a bank raid in Bushey, where £2500 was netted. But perhaps the most amazing thing was that someone had bothered to re-spray the bonnet of the car matt black, à la Viva GT. Obviously a criminally-minded Vauxhall enthusiast.

Here's Mr W. H. Pelling of Westcliff-on-sea taking delivery of the first Vauxhall 10. He'd been the first to place an order for the car without ever having seen one. Now that's what you call brand loyalty.

To Trent Harvard, Senior Marketing Executive with a major soap powder company the idea of giving away a car in a national competition was an inspired one. The winner wouldn't just get a car – they'd receive a customised Cresta.

Above the normal specification leather upholstery, sheepskin carpets, metalflake finish paintwork and extra chrome was included. Getting hold of a Cresta, then the sheep, wasn't a problem, but spangles! These sweets were included on the specification sheet because someone had specified a spangled rather than the technically accurate metalflake finish.

More than 1,500 packets of spangles were acquired wholesale by the coachbuilding company who agreed to prepare the car. Not surprisingly they thought it a bit strange, but followed their very specific orders nonetheless.

Making the spangles stick to the paintwork was a problem, although the vinyl roof provided the perfect surface. Trent was asked whether they should bother with the rest of the car and he gave his executive decision on that. No.

The following day the car was driven to London for the presentation to the lucky winner. Heavy traffic meant that Trent's last minute check couldn't be done and the Cresta driven straight to the Mayfair Hotel. However, it started to spit. Then rain. Then pour.

A rather sticky Cresta arrived outside the hotel. A rather distressed driver had to be chiselled out of the car! And Trent Harvard was looking for a new position. Not necessarily in marketing.

Watch out Beadle's about. Zany TV programme presenter Jeremy Beadle went too far with one of his own screen stunts.

The wizard wheeze involved spraying the victim's Vauxhall Cavalier a particularly horrific blue. Jeremy even had the agreement of Phillip Wiltshire's parents.

Phillip was taken in by the jape and was good-natured enough to laugh at it all. However, when it came to taking the blue gunk off, the original metallic finish was totally ruined by big white blotches.

The TV company had to stump up over £1,500 for a re-spray! So at least Phillip got the last laugh!

There is an entry in the alternative book of records for lifting an object with your teeth. And that record breaking lift by the "Great Gummo" was carried out on a Cavalier convertible. Therefore old Gummo took the strain of 2299 lb (1045 kg) between his choppers.

A doctor writes, "don't imitate this at home with your own Vauxhall."

CELEBRITY Vauxhalls

Famous Owners

Here's a few of Vauxhall's celebrity owners, who reveal why they like their cars.

Bonnie Langford

Dancer, singer, actress, it's actually quite difficult to avoid seeing Bonnie on TV or at the theatre. Successes like *Cats* and *The Pirates of Penzance* means that she's constantly on the move and in search of a parking space. To keep up with her hectic lifestyle she's got the perfect runabout in her Vauxhall Nova. The garage where she bought the Nova even customised it for her by incorporating her name in the yellow side stripe. (*Autocar & Motor*)

Murray Walker

For some reason a motor race without Murray Walker wouldn't be quite the same. His enthusiasm for the sport often means that he says things he doesn't quite mean, but that all adds to the fun. Having worked in advertising for many years and in particular on the Vauxhall account meant that he has owned a succession of Luton's finest products which includes a Viscount, Ventora and Victor Estates and more recently a Cavalier. The GTE was acquired to put the fun back into his day-to-day motoring. I think it's worked, as Murray describes it as a four-wheeled motorcycle. (*Autocar & Motor*)

Leslie Howard

One of the finest classical pianists in the world, Leslie Howard has worked hard at his craft. Well known on the concert circuit and in the recording studio his priorities mean that music always comes first. Therefore a £22,000 Steinway for practising purposes is essential, whilst a similarly expensive car isn't. However, the Viva does at least provide reliable transport even if it's more difficult to get a good tune out of. (*Autocar & Motor*)

Julian Lloyd Webber

For this world-renowned musician the biggest motor preoccupation is finding a car that can comfortably accommodate his cello. Whether it's the front seat, back seat or boot, Julian's Vauxhall Senator can easily swallow up several cellos at once. So far the Senator has proved to be swift and stylish transport between concerts. Previously Julian had used a number of General Motors products for cello duty, including a Manta and a Monza, as well as a succession of Minis!
(*Sunday Times*)

Archive Owners

George Bernard Shaw

He was a keen Vauxhall driver for seven years, and here is the postcard he sent to the Editor of the *Vauxhall Motorist Magazine* giving details, including selling price. Shaw was 91 when he penned this note!

From
Bernard Shaw

In reply to your 373/613/M/R dated the 24th

I drove a Vauxhall 23-60 h.p, (No. NK5563) from June 1923 to April 1930, when I sold it for £100 to a Mr Edwin James Grove of 369 Seven Sisters Road, South Tottenham N.15. It may be running still.

During the 7 years, it had plenty of hard use in England and on the continent, much of it over mountains. It was a first rate car, and seemed to me a marvel after years with a woolly old slow combustion machine of another make.

I have no objection to your using the photograph if you can get a decent print of it.

G.B.S.

4, Whitehall Court (130) London, S.W. 1.
Telegrams: Socialist, Parl.-London.
Telephone: Whitehall 3160.

Ayot Saint Lawrence, Welwyn, Herts. 27 Oct 1947
L. & N.E.R. Welwyn Garden City, 5 miles Wheathampstead 2½
Telegrams and Phone: Codicote 218.

NK·5563

Sir Alec Rose

Here being installed in a Viscount after another epic voyage. And when he did spend time on land, he did so at the helm of a Victor 101.

Jackie Charlton

Here 'Big Jack' kicks off the sports section of archive owners as he receives the keys to a 101 Deluxe after part-exchanging it against his old Victor. This photo was taken in 1965, which probably means that he was driving it at the time our boys won the cup. Is there any connection? After all, could Jack have been so commanding, yet composed in defence if he'd been motoring in something less comfortable or reliable?

Geoff Boycott

Arguably England's best cricketer, Geoffrey takes delivery in 1968 of a spanking new Victor. Whether the vehicle on the left is the part-exchange is open to question. Nice shot though of Geoff with a full head of hair.

Ray Illingworth

Another Yorkshire cricketing legend who also put his faith in a Victor. This time it's an FE with plenty of room for all that cricketing bric-à-brac.

Spotted with a Vauxhall

Eamonn Andrews

The Thames Television sponsored Firenza which was handed over on live TV to Eamonn Andrews. Can't spot him anywhere, but the unmistakable character on the left is of course Gerry Marshall.

George Formby

British film star, saucy songster and music hall artiste, George was quite prepared to do anything for a laugh, even squeeze into a pint-sized Vauxhall.

Sabu the Elephant Boy

Doing an excellent impression of a bonnet mascot, Sabu was a well-known film star in the '30s and as the publicity blurb claimed 'had an unusual power over elephants'.

Vauxhalls

have also turned up on dozens of TV shows. Here are the edited highlights. *Randall & Hopkirk Deceased* – The surviving private eye runs a white Ventora and the deceased's wife has a white Viva. *The Beidebecke Affair* – James Bolam's GPO surplus Bedford (Viva) van is the MOT borderline that takes him and Barbara Flynn on many jazz-inspired adventures. *The Avengers* – In an episode known as the 'Gravediggers' Steed (Patrick MacNee) is lucky enough to have a 30/98 at his disposal to help solve the mystery. *The Bill* – an undercover Cavalier is often used by the boys in blue. *Auf Wiedersehen Pet* – Barry's (Timothy Spall) Bedford (Viva) van is barely alive, but still gets him from job to job.

Take Your Pick

On that popular TV programme Michael Miles would courteously ask the contestant, 'Take the money, or open the box?'. The studio audience would of course try to help. In this case the unnamed winner made the right decision. What a lucky bloke to end up with a brand new Viva!

Jack Brabham

World Championship winning driver and constructor, who for a time, as the advertising put it, 'breathed' on Vivas. The result, apart from tasteful side stripes, was a boost to the performance.

110

James Hunt
Continuing the famous racing driver theme, James was heavily involved in promoting Luton's products during the '70s. Here he is tooling around in a Firenza Sport.

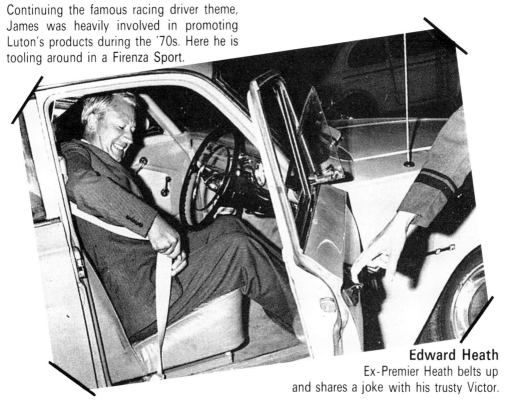

Edward Heath
Ex-Premier Heath belts up and shares a joke with his trusty Victor.

Eartha Kitt

Here trying a racing Firenza for size whilst
Gerry Marshall shamelessly attempts to steal
the limelight from the international singing
and acting star.

John Noakes

Take my word for it, John Noakes is behind
the wheel of this Viva. Recorded in action for
Blue Peter, he was leading
Gerry Marshall at

this point. Amazing
what a few old squeezy
bottles and bits of sticky backed
plastic will do.

George V

It was a D-type staff car that was chosen
during the First World War to take him across
the Flanders mud to Vimy Ridge.

Princess Margaret
Admires a 'Prince Henry' before climbing
aboard for a spin.

114

Duke of Edinburgh

Alights from a Victor, possibly from the appropriately named and trimmed VIP which is now extremely rare.

Royal Connection

As befitting a car that could count Rolls-Royce as its only serious rival in the early part of the century, Vauxhall's quality products have always found favour with the Royal family.

Prince Charles & Lord Mount-batten

Spotted taking a keen interest in a Viva GT.

VAUXHALL BITS AND PIECES

Most, least, strangest. Here's a bizarre collection of Vauxhall connected pix that frankly wouldn't fit comfortably into any other section of the book.

Most tipsy Vauxhall

I suppose it has to be 'Ye Olde Vauxhall Inn' somewhere in Surrey. I say somewhere, because my dedicated team of researchers rather lost their bearings after visiting the 23rd pub in the county that was called 'Ye Olde', and when they returned several days later, even the Surrey location was in some doubt. But apparently it was named after the gardens (see back – The Vauxhall Heritage), rather than the car.

Most tartan Viva

Here they are – the McDougall Girls. The promotional idea was to get as many bags of flour into as many households as possible. And what better way to it than with a bunch of mini-kilted lassies and Vivas with stick on McDougall Tartan. However, the first batch of panels featured the McDonald Tartan!! This almost earned the suppliers a Glasgow handshake (head butt) before the problem was rectified.

Floppiest Vauxhall

This is, in fact, an inflatable 'MW' Bedford truck which was produced by the Luton boffins during World War 2. It wasn't intended as a floating lorry, or anything as obvious as that. The intention was to deceive, and when viewed from above by the enemy that's exactly what it did. They thought all our troops and lorries were in one part of the country, when in reality they weren't. That's how we won.

Most psychedelic Viva

Yes, you guessed it. The date is 1967 and the villains are a bunch of art students. The Vauxhall dealer's angle was a bit of free publicity and the accolade of the most grooviest, hip, far out, guys in the car trade. Thankfully the custom paint job didn't stay on the car – it washed right off!

Most unusual delivery

The location is Accra on the Gold Coast of Africa. The date is about 1934. The occasion is the delivery of a large box with Vauxhall on the side. And on the inside lurks a Light Six convertible. In those days nothing was too much trouble, even taking your trusty Vauxhall on holiday with you.

Roomiest Vauxhall No1

With a boot so big you could hold a 'bring a bottle' party inside. A roof so wide a squadron of Harrier Jump Jets could settle down on it for a quick tea break without breaking formation. And a bonnet so long you could only see the wing mirrors on a clear day. The Viscount would seem to have won the roomiest car title hands down, but as you can see with only the driver on-board, it's looking a bit cramped already.

Roomiest Vauxhall No2

But once you turn to a Victor estate, things begin to look a bit more promising. Restricting themselves to the rear load space, 15 Vauxhall apprentices manage to cram inside. Soon after this picture was taken, SPACE (Society for the Protection of Apprentices in Cars Etc) was formed.

Roomiest Vauxhall No3

Another bunch of students, this time from Strathclyde University. The barely recognisable Vauxhall under those bodies is a 1949 Velox. The record of 33 was set in a good charity-raising cause. But I can only count 31.

The quickest Vauxhall to work

'The Cresta now leaving platform 4' – Wouldn't it be marvellous if we really could drive our Vauxhalls to work? This Cresta was put on the tracks for a Shell Petroleum television commercial. It obviously worked, but why wasn't a regular service introduced? The on-board cheese sandwiches couldn't have been any worse than what BR usually offer.

TO PROVE A POINT

121

Most distinctive number plates

Owning a registration plate that is worth more than the Vauxhall it's attached to, is just about impossible. However, a few years ago Michael James and his wife Janet were tooling around in a pair of identically finished cars, red paintwork with white vinyl roofs and reg numbers that were just a digit away from each other. You can probably think of a better James Bond gag than I can, so I won't bother.

Smallest Vauxhall

Dinky toys apart, the Rycraft Scoota Car must rank as the smallest driveable Vauxhall. Powered by a 1 hp engine situated behind the driver, it wasn't going to break any speed

Embarrassing Mayors. Oldham's first citizen compares the Rycraft with his official Vauxhall.

records. Costing £70 in 1935 it certainly wasn't a bargain, but in publicity terms, apart from underwhelming the odd stationary dray horse, it was incredibly successful.

Entertaining theatre-goers. Here the illusionist Mr. Christopher Charton prepares to 'vanish' both car and driver at the Grand Theatre, Derby.

Vaux. and Fox..

Now this is a bit more subtle. What you are witnessing is someone throwing themselves about on ice. Not just any old ice though, this is the Cresta run. Geddit?!?!

Worst Vauxhall 'Pun'

This is a close one. The first picture actually shows a tame fox called Reynard, perched on top of a DY.

Biggest Snoot gathering

In competition terms Thruxton in 1974 provided the venue for a one-off Firenza-only race that brought the largest gathering of Droops ever. Each car was sponsored by a Vauxhall dealer who was landed with the bodywork repair bill after the highly competitive race. More details in the Competition section. Otherwise, if you want to see a similar gathering of Vauxhall's rarest post-war car, you'd better join the Droop Snoot Group.

Most ridiculous publicity photo

No comment.

Nick Nick

Vauxhalls have always been amongst the forces' favourite pursuit vehicles. In the '30s it was the Light and Big Six.

Prototypes, one off's & specials

If every Vauxhall you see seems to be a Cavalier, here's a collection of rare and in some cases extinct cars to prove that over the years Luton's finest have come in all shapes, sizes and packages. In the early years it was possible to plonk some very odd things on top a Vauxhall chassis.

Handsome Cab

This was actually based on a 1905 Vauxhall. The idea for the car is attributed to Earl

Ranfurly who obviously felt that the classes should be kept as far apart as possible. Not surprisingly it wasn't a popular conversion.

Edwardians

Actually this was a fairly restrained example of Edwardian coachbuilding (circa 1910) for the monied classes. However, the chauffeur hadn't got any closer to proper weather protection.

Tank

It might resemble an armoured car, but this was a genuine attempt to build a cosy coupé. Cobbled together for T.W. Mays, father of famous racing driver Raymond, who really should have known better.

Bay window

The only thing that's missing from this one-off is double glazing and a pair of nets.

Motorcycle

Way back in 1924 Luton seriously considered building a two-wheeled Vauxhall! It was an advanced design with a 931 cc engine which was part of the same clutch and gearbox unit, with the rear wheel being driven by a shaft rather than a chain. In fact some of today's 'bikes aren't so advanced. In all just a half a dozen were produced. Only one is known to have survived, re-constructed from various genuine and reassembled parts in the '50s.

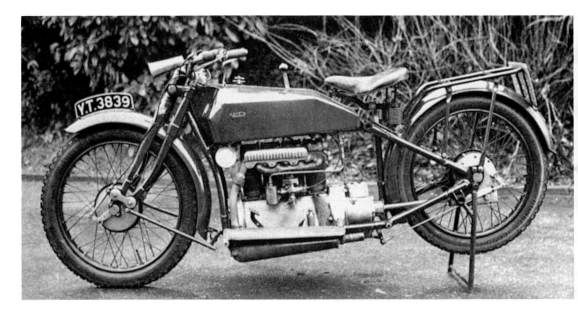

Drop Top 1

Not surprisingly the antipodeans enjoy pulling the top off almost anything, especially if it's a bottle, or as they call it, a tinny. Here they're letting the sun get to another type of tinny – a Velox. An essential beach accessory in the '50s with the barby following close behind. Converted by Holden, the year is 1953.

Drop Top 2

Placed in this sumptuous studio setting, probably the only place it wasn't raining, this Crayford-converted Viva really was a pretty-looking thing. These days finding one is almost impossible.

Wasp

Quite what this jacked up Viva was used for remains something of a mystery. The windscreen wiper suggests autocross. The sticker on the wing drag strip racing. About the only contest it could never have been suitable for was one of the beauty variety.

Dragster

A Chevette with a difference that actually ran quite regularly at Santa Pod Speedway and was officially sanctioned by DTV. Note the fibreglass body. In fact, during the '70s, turning otherwise quite sedate Vauxhalls into track burners was a popular pastime.

Apart from the VX4/90 nose this V8 monster had very little to do with Luton's products, although the pilot, Clive Skilton was a Vauxhall dealer.

Less radical, though no less exciting was this Victor Estate which actually has castors fitted to keep it moving whilst the front is airborne.

Customised

Vauxhalls have always been easy targets for customisers because if you got it all wrong there were always others to take its place as guinea pigs. These days anything less than a faithful ground-up restoration is regarded as sacrilege. A major hacksaw job on this '61 Cresta brought about a unique pick-up conversion.

Costin

Pictured with its aspiring owner, who has probably grown into it by now, the car was designed and built by Frank Costin, the 'cos' in Marcos. Called the Amigo, it sat on a wooden chassis and had Victor mechanics, which included the 1975 cc engine. In standard form it could exceed 130 mph. Just eight were built between 1970 and '71.

Panther Lima

Specialist car builders Panther decided in 1976 to broaden the appeal of their range with a low-cost sports car. Retaining the '30s and early '50s motoring spirit they installed the Magnum's 2.3 litre unit and used many other Vauxhall components. The powerful engine combined with such a light body meant very lively performance and made it into a modern Morgan. In the '80s it evolved into what is now known as the Kallista which has been the mainstay of the company's output ever since.

XVR

A brave Vauxhall design study from 1966 that made it from the drawing board, but sadly no further. There is quite a resemblance between it and that other famous GM product the Chevrolet Corvette. Another 'might-have-been' I'm afraid.

SRV

This styling Research Vehicle was first shown to the public in 1970. A full four seat car, it incorporated a number of advanced features aimed at improving safety. The rear engined layout, Vauxhall's first, could have spelt another supercar era for them. Ferrari might have had something to worry about if production had gone ahead.

Equus

A close relative of the Lima is Vauxhall's own Equus. Based on the same floor plan and using the 2.3 litre unit, this would have been Vauxhall's first sports car since the '30s. Making its debut at the 1978 Motor Show it attracted a great deal of attention, but it remained in prototype form. Who knows, it could nave rivalled the Toyota MR2 for appeal and become one of Britain's finest sports cars?

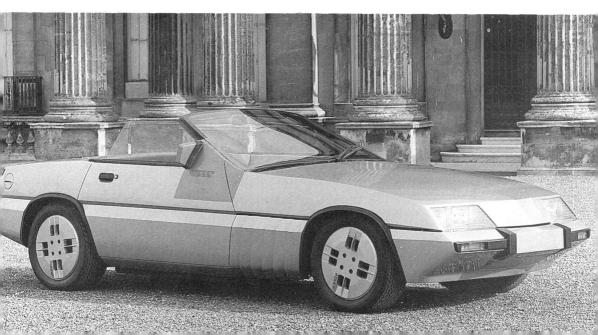

Silver Bullet

Brainchild of Wayne Cherry the Silver Bullet was also used as his day-to-day transport. This Droop differed from the unofficially released ones in that it sported six headlamps, a much lower rubber spoiler, full leather interior and unlike the tame sport-hatches had a rather more exciting 2.3 fuel injected unit with Getrag gearbox. Other subtle touches included a tinted glass sunroof, tartan door panels and all the dials and control symbols re-painted crimson to harmonise with the black and red interior. This car was rescued from the roof of the Vauxhall design studio by the Lindsay Brothers and fully restored.

Big Bertha

Without all the advertising and racing numbers old Bertha would have made one hell of a road car. In fact, that was the intention. The racer was to have been a prelude to the road version. Unfortunately the V8 Ventora was never to be, and Bertha was wrecked and reassembled as Baby Bertha.

Black Magic

Another Wayne Cherry runabout. This time the car was a Chevette, but not any old Chevette. The 2300 HS received the benefit of Cherry's DRG (down the road graphics) concept. This meant that it had to look good standing still. The additional fibreglass modifications included side skirts and spoilers and that full 'ground effect' look was achieved with extra rubber. Incorporated into the spoiler were additional driving lights and the indicators moved to the bumper. Inside, the tinted glass sunroof threw light on the leather sports seats, walnut dashboard and the innovative split rear seat.

Silver Aero

Vauxhall's first Turbo excursion powered 2.3 Cavalier Coupé with distinctive front-end styling which sadly never got further than this one-off.

FUTURE

The way your next Vauxhall will look is in the hands of one man, Wayne Cherry. He is Director of Design in Europe for General Motors, continuing the good work he started in Luton more than 20 years before. In all, more than 200 work at General Motors Europe Design, and Cherry oversees the small teams that are assigned to the various projects. Here are a few thoughts and possibilities.

An off-road Vauxhall? With the existence of the 4 x 4 Cavalier this technology could be utilised in a multi-purpose vehicle. Reflecting the corporate look of the current range it could even be badged as a Bedford. In fact, at the time this book was going to press there were reports that GM subsidiary Isuzu would have their 4 wheel drive Trooper built at Luton. So it could be a reality.

The Carlton and Senator always feature Vauxhall's most significant technological advances which are then included across the rest of the range soon after. This trend is likely to continue. These prestigious saloons will undoubtedly become more aerodynamic over the next few years.

A successor to Equus and the XVR? Not only should Vauxhall be producing advanced styling studies, they should be putting them on the road. An exciting roadster like this, mated to the new 16-valve power unit would boost their sporting image no end, and of course it would open up the convertible marketplace that Vauxhall successfully re-entered with the Astra and Cavalier drop tops.

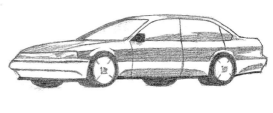

MOTOR SPORT

Things look as busy as ever for Vauxhall in the next few years. Their heavy commitment to rallying will continue with Derek Bell taking an even more active role and perhaps dedicating himself to this sport and retiring from the track. Of course he might still have the occasional outing in the Carlton Thunder-saloon which is going to keep us entertained for quite a long time to come in the successful hands of John Cleland and Vince Woodman.

Vauxhall is also committed to cultivating new racing talent. The AC Delco Astra-Nova Challenge has given the next generation of rally drivers the opportunity to prove themselves at the wheel of a 1300 Astra or Nova. Low in cost but high in excitement.

The Vauxhall Lotus Challenge does the same thing at a different level, but the implications are the same, as the drivers of tomorrow are given a chance today. But couldn't this also signal an entry into Formula 1? Why not? Although Lotus and Vauxhall are part of General Motors, Luton could still strike out on their own and into other single seat formulas. Remember Vauxhall took on track racing and international rallying without previous experience and proved to be highly successful.

Is this the next Cavalier? Seriously it could be. The car: General Motors Sunraycer.
The race: Inaugural transcontinental World Solar Challenge race in Australia. From Darwin to Adelaide – 1950 miles.
Winners: 44 hours 54 minutes at an average speed of 41 mph. The next finisher was 600 miles behind.
Gold: To keep the driver cool the canopy is gold-plated to reflect radiation.
Technological spin-off: This is the Magna-quench super strength, rare earth, iron-based permanent magnets mean that electric motors can now be much smaller and operate more efficiently than ever before. In fact the

137

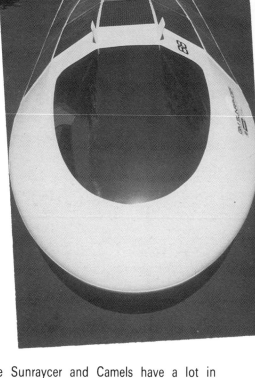

number of applications for a magnet that never loses its power is almost limitless.
Shape: Very low drag acheived using space technology.

SUNRAYCER SPECIFICATION

Seats: 1
Dimensions: Length – 19.7 ft; Width – 6.6 ft; Height – 3.3 ft
Chassis: Aluminium tube spaceframe
Body: Sandwich of Kevlar/Nomex
Wheels: 17 inch spoked wheels.
Suspension: Front – MacPherson struts; Rear – independent arms
Weight: 360 pounds
Solar panels: 90 sq. ft – 7,200 cells.
Motor: 3 kW, 4 hp Magnaquench brushless DC weighing 11 pounds.
Batteries: Silver zinc, 68 cells 102 volts.

The Sunraycer and Camels have a lot in common.

Camel:	Sunraycer:
Reliable but temperamental	Reliable
A few gallons of water every week	Driver needs the odd drink
Smells	No smells. Hammock seat maintains air circulation.

Even if it is a bit cloudy over here GM and Vauxhall have thought of that too. This is one of GM's experimental urban electric cars, a converted Chevrolet Chevette, renamed the Electrovette. Powered by a 240 volt lead acid battery pack housed behind the rear seats, the vette has a range of 40–50 miles at a top speed of 30 mph.

Within the modern confines of the General Motors Research Laboratories lies the technology for making Vauxhall's future happen. Here engineers and research scientists are constantly improving ways of designing and building cars.

Secure future

As this ad makes clear, pinching a Vauxhall is no laughing matter. The criminally minded amongst us have already discovered that there are security-coded radios, side profile cut keys with 2,000 combinations, deadlocks and no vulnerable door lock button.

Soon we won't even need keys to open up our Vauxhalls. Coded number entry, infrared beam locks and voice activated entry are all very real possibilities.

VAUXHALL. ASTRA.
Remember, we got here first.

GTE

B498 TYH

ASTRA. CAR OF THE YEAR, 1985.

"CAR OF THE YEAR" IS ORGANISED BY TELEGRAPH SUNDAY MAGAZINE, QUATTRORUOTE, AUTOVISIE, L'EQUIPE, STERN AND VI BILÄGARE

This is history, but it's surely not the last time Vauxhall will win such a coveted award. (n.b. Carlton Car of the Year 1987). The future looks bright for the little Griffin.

Owners' & enthusiasts' clubs

If you're fanatical about Vauxhalls and want to know more about them, help is at hand. In fact there are thousands of other enthusiasts all over the country who feel exactly the same way as you and they are all members of the many specialist Vauxhall clubs. You don't even have to be a Vauxhall owner, just absolutely nutty about the cars and everything that goes with them. Imagine whole weekends, looking around, talking about and arguing over Vauxhalls. Newsletters that keep you up to date with Vauxhall activities. As well as access to rare parts, special insurance schemes and discounts.

So here's a brief summary of the specialist clubs who cater for Vauxhalls. It's up to you to decide which club is right for your needs. Simply write to them and they will without obligation send you all the information that you'll need.

OPEL - VAUXHALL DRIVERS CLUB

This club was formed to cater for all post-war Vauxhalls.

Members can obtain parts at a significant discount. There is also a rare parts location service and a number of competitive insurance schemes. Technical advice by phone or letter is provided free of charge, and a list of Vauxhall specialists means that work is carried out cost-effectively to the highest possible standard. There's also a club magazine and regular bulletins to keep members fully up to date, including the GM Opel-Vauxhall sport magazine.

A full programme of national and local events include track tests, talks and rallies.

Contact: Vauxhall Drivers Club,
PO Box 8,
Dereham,
Norfolk.

141

'F' VICTOR OWNERS CLUB

Sports hatches and Chevette 2300HS.

Members receive four issues of their professionally produced *Droop Snoot Noos* which carries many features and a classified ad section. A spares scheme helps keep cars on the road. There's a comprehensive selection of club regalia, with meetings organised on a national and local basis.

Contact: 11 New Road,
              Sands,
              Bucks HP12 4LH.

This club was formed in 1981 to preserve and maintain the F, FB and Victor models only from 1957 to '64. Associate members are also very welcome.

The club offers free technical advice and a spares location service. There is also a full programme of national and local events, including a quarterly magazine. The 'Centre Section' of the magazine deals with problems that may occur with members' cars.

This is a particularly well organised club as it is responsible for the annual Vauxhall gathering at Billing Aquadrome.

Contact: Derek Holder,
              40 Gallows Hill Lane,
              Abbotts Langley
              Nr Watford,
              Herts.

PA ▽ PB ▽ PC ▽ E ▽ SERIES

OWNER'S CLUB

The Club caters for PA Velox, Cresta; PB Velox, Cresta; PC, Cresta, Viscount and E Wyvern, Velox, Cresta. In fact, all the big Vauxhalls from 1951–72.

Members get a quarterly magazine and regular newsletters to keep up to date on the many rallies and events that are organised by the club. Spares location, technical advice, club regalia and free advertising in the club magazine are just some of the services on offer.

Contact: Simon Walker,
              79 Framfield Road,
              Hanwell,
              London W7 1NQ.

DROOP SNOOT GROUP

This is the high performance Vauxhall club which covers the droop snoot Firenzas,

The Club was created for enthusiasts of FD and FE VX4/90s, but also embraces Victors, Ventoras and the later VX series.

Information is provided by a bi-monthly magazine which offers free advertising and keeps members posted about local and national events. The Club also offers technical advice, access to historical material (brochures etc) and has a policy of acquiring and locating spares.

Contact: 61, Stoke Road
Walton-on-Thames,
Surrey, KT12 3DD

Cars built between 1903 and 1957 are catered for by the club, although associate membership is available to those who don't own cars manufactured within that period.

Flute News keep members informed of everything that's going on, featuring owner's stories, free classified ads and details of the available Club regalia.

The Club is very concerned about preserving the Vauxhall motoring heritage and offers comprehensive technical and restoration advice.

Contact: 42 Deerfold,
Astley Village,
Chorley PR7 1UH

OWNERS CLUB

Not surprisingly the Club caters for all Vivas which means HA, HB, HC including vans and estates, all special models, such as convertibles and Brabhams and derivatives, Magnums, Firenzas etc.

A quarterly magazine contains a classified section, technical help, news of national and local events and details of the available club regalia.

Contact: Adrian Miller,
The Thatches,
Snetterton North End,
Snetterton,
Norwich, NR16 2LD.

Although aimed at the F, FB, FC 101 and FD Victors the club also embraces CA Bedford vehicles and welcomes all other Vauxhalls, from pre-war to present day.

A Club magazine gives details of the many events that they organise as well as members' features and technical advice. They have two spares departments and facilities to re-manufacture certain items.

Contact: Secretary,
12 Cliff Crescent,
Ellerdine,
Telford,
Shropshire TF6 6QS.

This is not a complete directory of every Vauxhall specialist but it should include at least one or two companies who may be able to help you find that elusive part, finish that attempted restoration and perhaps make it move just a little more quickly. The following symbols should help you quickly identify what they get up to:

OA – Performance
OB – Bodykits
OC – DIY kits
OD – Restoration
OE – Spares

Inclusion in this section does not necessarily imply recommendation of the companies concerned as neither author nor publisher will be aware of managerial changes, or policy after publication.

Vauxhall Parts Centre [OE]
39 Fulwell Road,
Teddington,
Middlesex TW11 0RH.
01 977 9925
Parts 1950–72

Sylva Autokits Ltd [OC[
18 Burrd Grove,
Lymington,
Hampshire SO41 9QR.
Sylva Striker Kit

Janspeed Engineering [OA]
Castle Road,
Salisbury,
Wiltshire SP1 3SQ.
0722 21833
Performance.

Irmscher UK [OA/OB]
2 & 4 Walhouse Road,
Walsall WS1 2BN
0922 720400
Tuning. Body Styling

Swindon Sportscars Ltd [OC]
Swanhill Garage,
Shrivenham,
Swindon SN6 8AS.
0793 783622
Sylva Leader Kit

Magard Limited [OA/OE]
372 East Park Road,
Leicester, LE5 5AY
0533 730831
Body kits. Performance parts.

Warren Kennedy Vauxhall Spares [OE]
Unit 16, Ross Trading Estate,
Greenfield Road, Pulloxhill,
Bedfordshire MK45 5ES
0525 718128/9

Courtenays Carquip UK [OA/OB]
Barroway Drove,
Downham Market,
Norfolk PE38 0AL
03668 318

Mumford Engineering [OC]
Gigg Mill,
Old Bristol Road,
Nailsworth,
Gloucestershire GL6 0JW.
Musketeer Kit

Blydenstein Racing Ltd [OA]
Station Works,
Shepreth,
Royston,
Herts SG8 6PZ
0763 60051
Performance.

DPR Forced Induction Systems Ltd [OA]
Water Coombe Lane,
Lynx West Trading Estate
Yeovil BA22 9JJ
Somerset
0935 32177
Supercharging.

Peter Maiden Components [OE]
Bodymoore Green Farm,
Coventry Road,
Kingsbury B78 2DZ
0827 874488

John Noble Engines [OA/OE]
Unit 18, Station Lane Ind Est,
Old Whittington,
Chesterfield.
0246 453867

MJ Matchen [OC]
The Garden,
Home End Crescent,
Ledbury,
Hereford,
Worcestershire
0531 2512
Hawk Wyvern Kit

P. O. Enterprises [OE]
1 Winston Drive,
Market Drayton,
Shropshire TE9 1RL
0630 3253
Parts

Rallyspares [OA/OE]
The Gardens Garage,
Hope Street,
Sandbach,
Cheshire CW11 0BB.
0270 760199

Obsolete Vauxhall Parts [OE]
30 Wheelwright Road,
Erdington,
Birmingham, B24 8NY.
021 382 8994
Parts

MARQUE CHART

Now if you wondered what model replaced which and when, these Vauxhall Marque Charts should help. They could even settle an argument with a fellow Vauxhall fanatic. On second thoughts though, they might even start several nasty incidents if my research is wrong.

I've put in as much detail as possible without bogging you down with every single version or derivative. But make sure that you take notes because questions may be asked later during the Trivia Test.

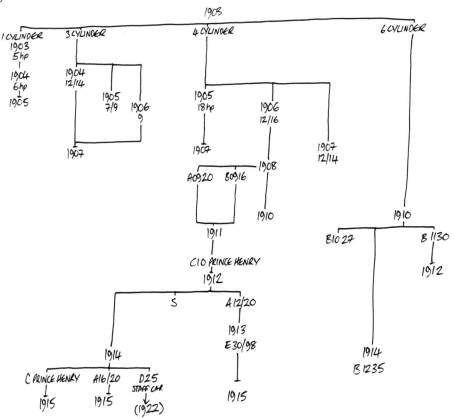

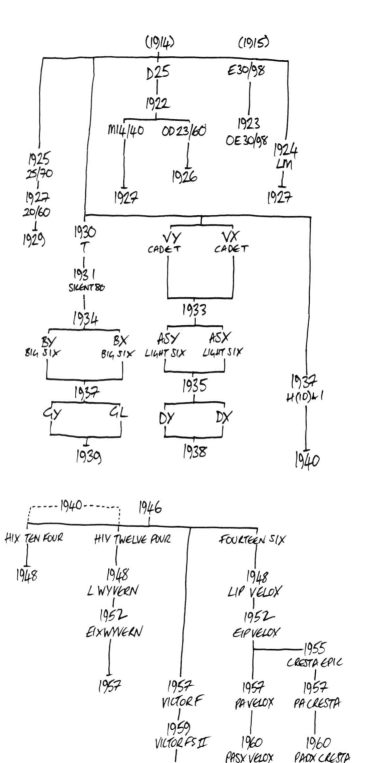

(1914)
(1915)

D25
E30/98

1922
1923
OE30/98

MI4/40   OD23/60
1924
LM

1925
25/70
1926

1927
20/60
1927
1927

1929)

1930
T
VY   VX
CADET   CADET

1931
SILENT 80

1934
1933

BY   BX   ASY   ASX
BIG SIX   BIG SIX   LIGHT SIX   LIGHT SIX

1937
1935
1937
H(10)4 1

GY   GL   DY   DX

1939
1938
1940

---- 1940 ----   1946

HIX TEN FOUR   HIV TWELVE FOUR   FOURTEEN SIX

1948
1948
L WYVERN
1948
LIP VELOX

1952
EIXWYVERN
1952
EIP VELOX

1955
CRESTA EPIC

1957
1957
VICTOR F
1957
PA VELOX
1957
PA CRESTA

1959
VICTOR FS II
1960
PASX VELOX
1960
PADX CRESTA

1962
VICTOR FB
1962
PB VELOX
1962
PB CRESTA

VX4/90

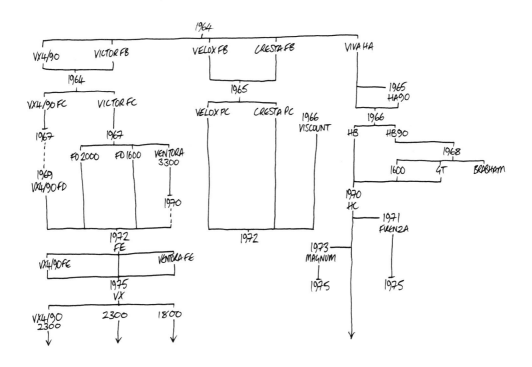

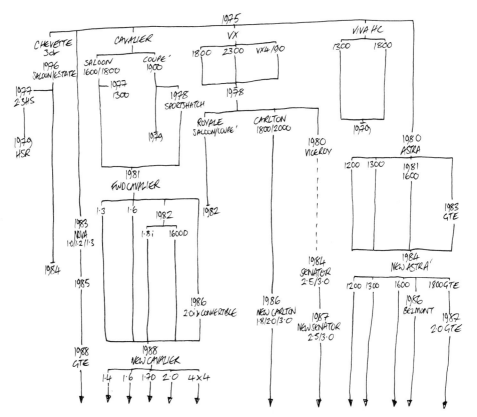

VAUXHALL

QUIZ TRIVIA

Here it is, the moment you've been waiting for – the end of the book. However, it isn't quite over yet. Why not pit your wits against Professor Gustav Foresight who came up with this brain tickling quiz. All the teasers contained here are based on the information contained in the Vauxhall Driver's Book, so there are no excuses.

1. True or false? (i) Gary Glitter is a direct descendant of Fulk Le Bréant (ii) The 30/98 was the first car sold with a guaranteed 100 mph top speed (iii) The fluted bonnet was retained as a design feature after the front of a prototype was damaged in an NCP car park.

2. Identify these cars

a.

3.

(i) What is this woman driving and

(ii) where has she just emerged from?

C.

5.   Vauxhall Algebra

+

X

–

= ?

6.   Why are these men looking so pleased
with themselves?

7. Complete the nicknames:
(a) Silver . . . . .
(b) Silver . . . . .
(c) . . . . . Magic
(d) Old . . . . .
(e) . . . . . Bertha

8.

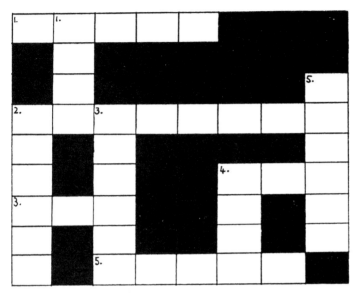

Across
1. Funny Front
2. Laughable saloon
3. 50s affliction
4. Beagle.
5. Well Conn*ct*d

Down
1. Super Star
2. Designer on top
3. Champion
4. Olé
5. Singer (see 5 across)

9. What's the connection between these two?

10. What comes next?   (i)
                               (ii)
                               (iii)

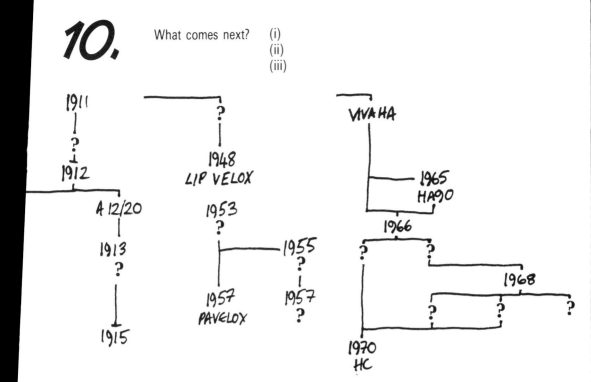

1911
?
1912
A 12/20
1913
?
1915

?
1948
LIP VELOX
1953
?
1955
?
1957
PAVELOX   1957
?

VIVA HA
1965
HA90
1966
?   ?
1968
?   ?   ?
1970
HC

(overleaf for ✓ or ✗)

THE SOLUTIONS

How to score. One mark for each correct answer which includes a mark for each sub-question and every crossword line you solve.

1. (i) False. (ii) True. (iii) Very false.
2. (a) Costin (b) Yes I know there's an Allegro in the background but you'll only score points if you spotted the Slyva Kit Car (c) Equus prototype sports car
3. (i) Ryecraft Scootacar and (ii) she has emerged from a miniature Mersey Tunnel
4. You ought to be able to spot Wendy Craig, Ed Stewart, Nicholas Parsons, Gerald Harper, Edward Woodward, Jack Douglas, Diana Coupland and Gayle Hunnicut. Anyone else scores a bonus mark and that shadowy, sinister, sunglasses-wearing figure at the back is of course Gerry Marshall.

5. $30/98 + 4/90 \times 10 - 90 = 35790$
6. They had swept the saloon car titles in 1971. Clever Dick marks for adding the titles – Irish Saloon Car Champion, Hill Climb Champion, Scottish Saloon Car Champion and Special Saloon Car Champion.
7. (a) Bullit (b) Aero (c) Black (d) Nail (e) Big

8.

¹S	¹N	O	O	T		
	O					
	V					⁵P
²C	A	³V	A	L	I	E	R
H		I					R
E		C			⁴V	A	N	C
³R	O	T			I			E
R		O			V			
Y		⁵R	O	Y	A	L	

9. They are both fighters. One's a
    Musketeer and the other's a Cavalier.

10

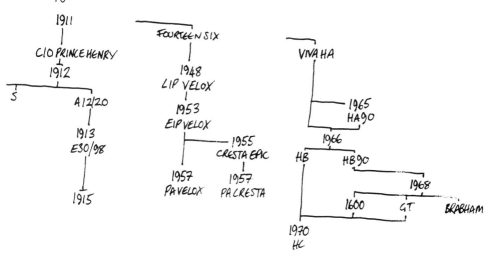

How did you score and what does it all mean?

0 – 15 Seek medical attention. You really can do a lot better than this. Back to page one.

15 – 30 Congratulations, you're not as stupid as you look. A respectable score, but you're certainly no Einstein. Make sure you take notes next time you take the Vauxhall Driver's Book off the shelf.

30 + Cheat. If not, your head is likely to have trouble negotiating doorways, Re-read the book, but don't pay too much attention this time.

Vauxhall Trivia Test © Professor G. Foresight.

It's often difficult to keep up with the pace of change in the motor industry and this book is no exception. Between completion and publication there have been new models, products and developments. Here's a selection of the most important events that give valuable pointers to the future of Vauxhall cars.

Vauxhall Calibra Sports Coupe

Perhaps the most exciting new car to come from Vauxhall since the Prince Henrys. Designed by Wayne Cherry this coupé hatchback fits on the Cavalier's floorplan making it a geniune four-seater. Although it is an obvious replacement for the Opel Manta and Monza, with a 16-valve turbocharged, 2 litre unit developed by Lotus, it packs a 200 bhp punch and a 150 mph top speed; the Calibra is a very different car. Rumours suggest that a Lotus badged version will be available by 1991 with the Lotus Carlton's power plant (see below). Four-wheel drive is also likely to be part of the specification soon.

Making its debut at the Motor Show in London, the Calibra will go on sale early in 1990 and set the standard for all coupés that follow.

Lotus Carlton

This is a totally reworked limited edition Carlton which is one of the most powerful saloon cars in the world. Developed by GM engineers in association with Lotus, the sports car manufacturer's expertise is felt most noticeably beneath the bonnet.

The engine is an all-new 3.6 litre six-cylinder engine with 24-valves and twin turbochargers. There is also a specially developed clutch and a six-speed manual gearbox to handle the incredible 360 bhp. To protect the environment, there are two closed-loop metal catalytic converters.

On the outside there is a full body kit, exclusively finished in metallic green with a rear spoiler that extends at speeds in excess of 100 mph, to further reduce lift. Inside, Connolly leather and electric sports seats make it luxurious yet functional.

Conclusion, watch out BMW and Jaguar!

Irmscher Cavalier

To complement the new style Cavalier. Irmscher have produced a body kit and performance package to make it an even more attractive proposition. Front spoiler, grille, side skirts, rear spoiler and rear door panel make up the body mods. Stiffer suspension, alloy wheels, twin exhaust and uprated engine change the on-road characteristics.

Vauxhall Gifts !!!!

If you want to drop hints for Christmas, or birthdays why not leave this page open for friends or family to stumble across. It almost seems too good to be true, but here they are, a complete range of Griffin badged products, from cuff-links to personal organisers and even pewter tankards.

More details from your Vauxhall dealer.

KEY:
1. Leather belt
2. Business card holder
3. Credit card holder
4. Gents wallet
5. Ladies wallet
6. Ladies jewellery roll
7. Personal organiser
8. Cufflinks
9. Tietack/lapel badge
10. Calculator
11. Digital alarm clock – Vauxhall
12. Digital alarm clock – Bedford
13. Reverso clock/calculator
 * Analogue alarm clock – Vauxhall
 * Analogue alarm clock – Bedford
14. Parker Vector roller ball pen
15. Edding 1700 fibre tip pen – Vauxhall
 * Edding 1700 fibre tip pen – Bedford
16. Cross pen/pencil set
17. Jotter block holder and block – Vauxhall
 * Jotter block holder and block – Bedford
18. Post-it note tray – Vauxhall
 * Post-it note tray – Bedford
 * Jotter block refill
 * Post-it refill
19. Magnetic tax disc holder
20. Electronic 'Trigger' lighter
21. Disposable lighter – Vauxhall
22. Disposable lighter – Bedford
23. Metal advertising paper clips
24. Pyramid and clips
25. Childrens puzzle
26. Swiss Army penknife – Bedford
27. Pocket torch
28. Set of darts in holder – Bedford
 * Set of flights
29. Conference/staff badges
30. Coasters – set of 6
31. Model Astra car
32. Red, white and
 silver/grey balloons – Vauxhall
33. Red, white and
 blue balloons – Bedford
34. White mug – Vauxhall
 * White mug – Bedford
35. GTE holdall
36. Pewter tankard
37. Golf umbrella

 * *Item available but not illustrated*

For comprehensive details, part numbers and prices please see accompanying list.

General Motors Service Parts Operations – UK, Dunstable, Beds., LU5 4LU.